FOUND MONEY ROADMAP

THE SMALL BUSINESS OWNER'S GUIDE TO INCREASING CASH FLOW, BOOSTING NET PROFIT, AND HAVING MORE FUN!

STEVE WILKINGHOFF

Copyright © 2017 Steve Wilkinghoff

All rights reserved. No part of this book may be used or reproduced in any manner whatsoever without the written permission of the author.

This book is dedicated to Sherri, Julia, Lauryn, Graeme, and Carter.

You guys make my life so rewarding, fun, interesting, and sometimes challenging. But always full of love.

Thank you each for being such special anchors in a crazy world.

Praise From Readers

Steve's first book, Found Money, blew me out of the water! I immediately ordered copies for all my staff and we used it in coaching our franchisees. Sequels don't always live up to the first book, but Found Money Roadmap is a strong exception! Steve not only clearly explains what drives a business to profitability and funds your dream lifestyle, but he gives you practical steps and worksheets that allow you to customize it to you and your business. It's a must-read for small business owners!

CHERYL HAMMONS, CFE, CSA
SENIOR VICE PRESIDENT, FRANCHISE SERVICES,
Home Helpers Home Care

Listen to Steve Wilkinghoff, one of the most important storytellers you have ever had the privilege to meet. I did. And my life has never been the same since.

MICHAEL E. GERBER
AUTHOR OF *THE E-MYTH REVISTED, AWAKENING THE ENTREPRENEUR WITHIN*, FOUNDER AND CEO
The Entrepreneur Capital Corporation

Steve is a motivational entrepreneur -- he'll give you perspective and make you realize you're business struggles are not uncommon. He will help you examine your business model through fresh eyes to revamp and direct your business decisions so that you can finally realize that dream lifestyle you always intended your entrepreneurial spirit to deliver.

STACIE BEEVER
Strategic Funding and Contract Management
Delco Automation Integrated Solutions

Solid tools and methods to analyze small to mid size businesses. It shows owners what to look for, and most importantly, how to make "great" decisions and grow more profitable.

CHIA-LI CHIEN, CFP, PMP
CEO and FOUNDER,
Value Growth Institute

"How does your business make money?" I guarantee that many of you don't actually know. If you did, you would be a millionaire, or even a billionaire right now — wouldn't you? I am not totally excluding myself here either. The key is to find a way that will yield the best results, constantly and continuously.

WILL FRANCO
MANAGING DIRECTOR
jiveSYSTEMS

If someone had told me that I would be THIS excited about finance and accounting book, I would have probably let out a big fat raspberry sound. This has to be the MOST FUN I've had reading about this topic – EVER. The style and tone through this whole book is so light, so personable and so friendly that you'll find yourself tearing through this content at lightning speed. Business owners and managers who have P&L responsibility will learn about the critical profit drivers that affect their business. You also will learn how to get your employees excited and engaged about the financial drivers that impact profitability.

IVANA TAYLOR
PRESIDENT
Third Force, Inc.

Steve's approach, tools, and tactics are guaranteed to show you how to unleash your hidden financial performance and then use it to create better financial results.

MARK CHERRYHOLMES
PRESIDENT,
BattleWagon Mounts, LLC

Great book. What an enlightening approach in addressing finance! By understanding the challenges of business owners, you knew exactly how to educate and inspire the reader. This relevant approach will ensure everyone who reads the book walks away with great insights on how to better their business.

RYAN TOWNEND
CEO,
William Joseph Communications

Found Money Roadmap teaches small business owners how to ensure consistent, predictable, profits by identifying and eliminating non-value added activities. It then shows how to use process-driven tactics and systems so your business provides the lifestyle you choose for you and your family.

TOM too tall CUNNINGHAM
Napoleon Hill Foundation Certified Instructor, Creator of the Journeys To Success book series

This book is easily going to be one of the first things I recommend ALL my clients read. If you want to "find" more profit in your business, Steve can show you the way!

ELY DELANEY
Automated Marketing Architect
YourMarketingUniversity.com

Finally, someone can show you what's really going on inside your business -- and why your profits never seem to add up to as much as you thought they would.

Steve Wilkinghoff gives you the "missing links" between the financial results you've been getting, the financial results you want, and how to bring them both together.

Steve's approach and the information he gives you in this book make it possible to get control of your financial results and create a MACHINE that predictably and dependably churns out the profits you want and need from your business.

KEVIN DONLIN
Marketing Optimizer + Copywriter
Client Cloning Systems

Found Money Roadmap shows you how to "put your business back to work again" and then gives you the tools – thanks Steve. By following these principles and the roadmap within you can create better and more dependable financial results from your business. In no time at all you'll be able to put your business to work for you, your team, and your community.

DAVID E. PERRY
Author of 'Hiring Greatness: How to Recruit Your Dream Team and Crush the Competition' and 'Executive Recruiting for Dummies'

CONTENTS

Introduction 10

Chapter 1 - The True Purpose of Your Business.......................1

Chapter 2 – Identifying YOUR Dream Lifestyle 11

Chapter 3 – The Found Money Wheel..................................21

Chapter 4 – When Does Your Business Actually Make Money?
....35

Chapter 5 – Is YOUR Business Making Money? 55

Chapter 6 – The PROCESS Of Net Profit 65

Chapter 7 – Gross Profit 101 79

Chapter 8 – The Found Money Gross Profit Formula..............85

Chapter 9 – Your Found Money Breakeven.........................101

Chapter 10 – Your Customer Profitability Map 109

Chapter 11 – Analyzing Your Customer Profitability Map 121

Chapter 12 – CSF's, KPI's, and QuickFailing for Success 133

INTRODUCTION

I'm a geek – I proudly admit it.

What I geek-out over is small business. I happily spend countless hours thinking about, talking about and 'looking about' for any small business led by a switched-on entrepreneur.

And when I find them I go full-on geek. I get so excited about helping them find the hidden financial performance in their business.

Over the years, however, uncovering hidden financial performance has become much more than a passion of mine. It has become a personal mission - my way to change the world.

Sound overly dramatic?

The fact is that small business owners around the globe are the true engine of the global economy. They are the vehicles for change, economic prosperity, climate and environmental leadership, and making the world a better place for everyone.

When a small business uncorks its hidden financial potential amazing things begin to happen.

The business owner suddenly becomes more relaxed and less stressed about their financial results. They are more confident that they can grow, defend, and prosper in any economy.

They can also compensate their team members with living wages and security along with fulfilling and meaningful work and working conditions.

These things contribute to a more relaxed family and home life (for both the owners and the team members). More quality time within each family – time spent in various activities, bonding, and improving the cohesiveness of the family.

This in turn leads to the ability to contribute more-fully in the community. In churches, schools, non-profit organizations, and other groups.

This leads to better communities, better regions, better nations, and a better world.

I've had my shares of ups and downs in business through the years. Through it all, Sherri, Julia, Lauryn, Graeme, and Carter have always been amazingly supportive. Often making sacrifices that were way beyond what they should have had to sacrifice.

This means that I know, firsthand, the miracle that can happen when we uncover hidden financial performance in our businesses. I also know how stressful it is when the pressure is on because of financial results that come up short of what we want.

So yes. My passion at geeking out over business has become a mission so we can all live better, be better, and make the world better.

Join with me on this mission and let's help change and improve the world together.

-- **Steve Wilkinghoff**

Chapter 1 - The True Purpose of Your Business

Since you're reading this book, odds are high that you're either a small business owner or someone who cares about one. Either way, it's critical that you have a crystal clear picture in your mind of why the business you care about exists.

Over the last 25 years as I've interacted with thousands of business owners I've come to realize there is often confusion in this area.

So that's where we need to start. Let's kill the confusion and look at the correct answer to the question, "What is the true purpose of your business?"

Same Question, Same Answers

I often ask entrepreneurs what the purpose of their business is. Invariably I get answers similar to:

- I love what I do, and wanted to make a living at it;
- I wanted to be rewarded for how hard I work;
- We help people;
- We provide a valuable product or service;
- I like to make my customers happy;
- I enjoy improving my customers' lives;
- People need what we sell;
- I can't imagine doing anything else;
- I have a hard time working for someone else; or
- I enjoy being in control of my future;

Every single one of these answers and their variations are wonderful goals and positive beliefs. But as reasons for your business to exist, they are all completely....

...WRONG!!!!!

It's not that these things are wrong to want and aspire to. In fact, those things are all very noble and wonderful – they are **fantastic** things to want to do and accomplish.

In fact, our world is a made a better place *because* people want to do these things. Just think about what society would look like if people didn't think like that.

We'd all be in trouble.

So I'm not against those things at all – as goals and beliefs.

But when it comes to reasons for a business to exist – they are just plain **WRONG!!** In fact they are useless. They just don't cut it.

When you make the mistake of thinking any of these things are reasons for your business to exist, one of two things will happen – neither good:

1. You get trapped in a hellish lifestyle. Where you work way too hard in your business and yet simply manage to make a living – just getting by. You end up sacrificing

your physical and emotional health. You sacrifice important relationships with your family and friends.

You struggle to get everything done that needs doing, and no matter how hard you work you just never seem to get caught up.

You end up overworked, stressed, unhappy, unhealthy, and burned-out. And the worst part is that, despite all your effort and sacrifices, you don't generate any real wealth for yourself and your family.

You end up with nothing more than a "job". A job that **you** have created for yourself.

And it's the worst kind of job. It gives you a low-paying position (in fact, often below minimum wage for the hours you devote), a punishing workload, almost unlimited risk and little (if any) freedom or flexibility to get away to relax, enjoy yourself, and connect with your family and friends.

OR...

2. Even worse, you discover that despite your worthy goals (helping others, etc.) your business simply isn't viable. No matter how hard you seem to work, it doesn't make enough money and cash flow to continue operating.

   Despite your desire to help others and provide them with something of value, your business simply can't sustain itself. You end up putting more and more money into the business. Eroding more and more of your wealth and personal net worth as time goes on.

Obviously neither of these situations is something you want to experience. Paradoxically, however, if you're like most small business owners you may find yourself in one (or both) of those scenarios at this very moment.

So What <u>IS</u> The Purpose Of Your Business?

To make money. End of story.

Really. That's it.

Why is making money the most important thing for your business to do?

The reason is that everything your business does (or could do) comes from its ability to make money. It's only after your business makes money that you have *options* for what to do with that money and your time.

Once you've created a business that makes money you can do one, some, or all of the following:
- Help people by using the money your business makes;
- Help more people by expanding your business;
- Work less by hiring some talented team members to make money when you aren't there;
- Travel;
- Increase your skills and knowledge in your area of expertise;
- Develop a new area of expertise;
- Start another business with money produced by the present business;
- Help improve the environment and your community;
- And whatever else you desire in your dream lifestyle.

How Much Money?

That depends on you.

It depends on you because to be truly successful your business must make enough money to enable you to live your Dream Lifestyle. 'Dream Lifestyle' is a very personal thing and is different for each business owner. Your Dream Lifestyle is so important that we will talk about it in detail in the next chapter.

Let's look at the story of Tom Golisano as example.

In 1971, Tom founded the company called Paychex, Inc. Under his guidance and with his energy, the company grew into one that now employs more than 12,000 people and has 100 offices across the United States.

That's exciting in it's own right.

But what makes Tom's story amazing is what he has done with the success of his company and how that success allows him to fulfill his Dream Lifestyle.

With the success of Paychex, Tom created the Golisano Foundation in 1985 with his own money. Today the foundation manages assets of roughly $25 million and provides opportunities for individuals with intellectual disabilities and offers support for their families.

In addition to the support Tom personally provides his own foundation, he generously supports many other organizations. In fact, since 1990, Tom has provided over $260 million in philanthropic contributions.

In addition to his philanthropic activities Tom also, at one time, own the professional hockey team, the Buffalo Sabres.[1]

Tom's passion for his community and the causes he believes in are uniquely actualized because he built his company into one that makes money. Enough money for himself, his employees, his community, and for those who benefit from his passion for helping others.

That's the power of creating a business that makes enough money and provides enough profit and cash flow to serve your Dream Lifestyle.

Acting Like You're NOT Supposed To Make Money

So, the purpose of your business is to make money – enough money to allow you to live your Dream Lifestyle. It is only when that happens that you truly have a stable, secure, sustainable, fun, and life-changing business.

ANYTHING you want that will make your business more fun, less stressful, more enjoyable – anything – depends on it making enough money to do those things.

Do you want your business to provide employment to your employees and their families? Great! But it absolutely WON'T do that for long if it doesn't make enough money.

Do you want your business to let you donate to your church, contribute to a charity, help others less fortunate, or other worthwhile causes? Great! But that simply WON'T be possible if it doesn't make money first of all.

---

[1] Golisano Foundation; http://www.golisanofoundation.org/tomGolisano.html

And donating to worthwhile causes IS NOT what your *business* is supposed to do. That's what *YOU* are **able to do**, as part of your Dream Lifestyle, **IF** your business makes the money it needs to make so that you can do it.

This probably seems simple and obvious. As simple and obvious as it seems, however, most business owners don't **act** like their business is supposed to make money for them.

In fact, most business owners actually do things in their business that make it seem like its purpose is to **NOT** make money.

They do activities that cost more than they return.

They create and sell products and services that don't create enough money for the business.

They chase customers that make less money for them than other customers that they tend to ignore.

They don't capture all the revenue and profit they could (and should) from their existing customers.

They add to their overhead expenses believing that adding resources like more team members will help them scale up and make more money.

The list could go on for pages. In fact, most business owners literally take hundreds of actions and make just as many decisions that it would make an alien from outer space who came to observe them believe that the purpose of their business was actually to NOT to make too much money.

But It Doesn't Have To Be That Way

In fact, it can't be that way. It can't be that way if you are serious about creating your Dream Lifestyle and having your business be the vehicle that makes that happen.

In fact, to get into the habit of examining each part of your business with a critical eye toward making money, try this little exercise.

Imagine that you are a space alien visiting earth from another planet and that you have come to earth to observe humans and have been assigned to closely observe "you" in your business.

Your alien commander has assigned you the job of carefully noting the way humans run businesses as part of a study of inter-planetary species.

If you were that alien, what things would you observe that make absolutely no sense to an objective, outside observer.

[Note that you can get additional copies of this worksheet and the other worksheets in this book by going to www.FoundMoneyRoadmap.com

Think all the "things" you do in your business that you know, deep down, just don't make much sense (like dealing with customers who grind you on prices, or are slow to pay, for example).

In the space provided write the report to your "alien commander" about what you would observe. List as many observations as you can think of:

Observations of Earthling That Appear To Make No Sense...	Why do you believe the Earthling does these things?

To be fair in reporting back to your "alien commander", **write a brief report about the things you would observe that seem completely logical.** List as many as you can think of:

Observations of Earthling That Seem Completely Logical...	Why do you believe the Earthling does these things?

Chapter 2 – Identifying YOUR Dream Lifestyle

The purpose of your business is to make money. Enough money to allow you to fund your Dream Lifestyle.

Of course, the concept of "Dream Lifestyle" means vastly different things to different people. To some people it means having enough money to contribute to worthy causes such as charities, church, and community.

For other people it means being able to take a massive amount of vacation time and having the money to enjoy some amazing experiences with their family, friends and loved ones.

At the end of each of those definitions of Dream Lifestyle, however, is money.

And if your business isn't making enough money for you to live your Dream Lifestyle it is failing. It is failing to live up to its true purpose and potential.

History Should Repeat Itself

The history of commerce is all about businesses being created to make money. The basis of early commerce was to facilitate the trading of goods and services for money that could then be used to purchase other goods and services.

Imagine an artist trying to survive and thrive in those early days of commerce. Could he eat his paint? Eat his canvas? Eat his brushes? Could he feed them to his family?

Of course not.

But he still had to support himself and be able to feed his family.

Starving Artists

So the artist had to become good at providing paintings people **wanted and would pay money for**. Those paintings had to be ones that people would pay enough money for so that he could cover his costs and have enough left over to buy what he and his family needed.

Making money, therefore, was the painter's primary goal for the business.

Art enthusiasts will want to talk about the importance of aesthetics and painting things that truly "moved" the artist. Those things <u>are</u> important and great to have in the artist's work.

At the end of the day, however, that was secondary for our artist. The first thing he had to do was paint in order to make money – if he wanted to eat and provide for his family.

If he painted often enough, and well enough, he was able to make enough money to provide for himself and his family AND still have time to devote to the "purer" forms of painting.

Back To The Future

Now bring your focus back to the present and think about yourself and your business.

You are likely passionate about what you do in your business and the products and services your business provides. Hopefully you are <u>completely</u> passionate about your business and the things it does because it's a miserable grind if your business doesn't turn you on every single day.

Passion becomes painful and hollow, however, if your business doesn't also make enough money.

Don't Work For Peanuts – Unless You're An Elephant

There are millions of small businesses in the world that pay their owners a good wage. But at the same time, a great number of them have their owners trapped in a lifestyle of hard work, and long hours.

They are on a seemingly endless treadmill where the owner works hard and "gets by" but just can't seem to ever really get the time or money to truly live their Dream Lifestyle.

They can't quite seem to make enough money to truly be relaxed about their financial results. Maybe they can't quite seem to get enough money so they don't have to worry about their children's education. Maybe they can't quite seem to get enough to pay down some debt or finally buy that vacation property.

Those kinds of businesses, while they may be viewed as being outwardly successful by others, are actually failing. They are failing at providing a secure and worry-free life for their owners. On that basis, no matter how long the business has been around or how successful others may view it – it's still failing because the owner isn't able to be free to live their Dream Lifestyle.

Unless your business allows you to fully realize your Dream Lifestyle, and create financial results that are dependable, predictable, and sustainable – it is a failure at its true purpose.

It's a failure because it is impossible for you to continue in such a business without eventually suffering damage – emotionally, financially, relationship-wise, or some other damage.

It isn't sustainable; it's subject to economic conditions; it's subject to your competitors; it's subject to your customers; and it's subject to a whole host of outside forces that rob you of control over your financial results.

"That's Our Paper Daddy"...

Let me tell you a personal story that happened to me early in my career as a business owner. This is a personal example of an outwardly successful business actually failing because it wasn't supporting its owner's Dream Lifestyle.

My business was about four years old at the time and I was working a ton. I was working hard as it grew - keeping up with the workload, changing systems, adding team members, and meeting new customers as the business continued to grow.

One night I zipped home for a quick dinner before heading back to the office to keep working into the night – a pattern that had become a habit as the business grew. When I got home, I went into the basement playroom to say hello to my kids.

They were fully engrossed in a game and seemed to be having so much fun I decided to just quietly watch for a bit. My two daughters had a brown paper poster taped to their little playhouse. They seemed to be excited with it and were busy talking to it, dancing around it, giggling with it, and having a great time.

I couldn't resist how cute the whole scene was any longer so I let them know I was home. After our hugs I asked what they were playing.

They both smiled proudly, and told me that they had made themselves a "paper daddy" so they could play with it since I wasn't around much.

They meant it in the truthful, innocent way that kids have. And they were proud of the fact that they had made it.

But while they were excited, I felt like I had just been punched hard in the stomach.

I had been so focused on working hard and spending time to keep the business going and growing that I had lost sight of the fact that my business was actually failing.

It was failing because it had become something that was taking me further and further away from the things that were truly important in life. Things like being around to spend time with my growing family and be an active part of their lives.

Millions Of Elephants – Everywhere There Are Businesses!

Most business owners allow themselves to become Takers – simply toiling away forever in the business and "taking" whatever it will send their way.

- They "take" whatever amount of money the business gives them.

- They "take" whatever vacation time their business gives them.

- They "take" whatever workload their business gives them.

And they continue doing that over and over, day after day, week after week, month after month, grueling year after grueling year. Until they finally give up, get sick, or die.

The vast majority of business owners are trapped by their business. They have allowed themselves to become servants to the business instead of having the business serve them.

Many business owners are feeling so beat up and so emotionally drained by the business that they would quit (or least seriously consider it) it they were given a viable opportunity to do that.

If they could find someone to take over their business and let them pay off any debt so they could "break even," they'd be out of there. But who the heck would buy their business?

Who, in their right mind, would pay ANYTHING just so they could take the business owner's place and start suffering so they wouldn't have to?

Even if a business owner could find someone else who would buy their business and allow them to "break even" they would still end up losing out.

When you consider that:
- "breaking even" means that all they received for their years of hard work was the "wage" they managed to earn while owning the business, and
- many business owners end up taking a wage less than the "market value" for their effort, talents, AND RISK,

...then the owner didn't really break even at all.

Tragically, they would actually have **managed to destroy wealth over the years they owned the business**.

Destroyed Wealth?

They have destroyed wealth because they would have been better off if they had worked that hard and got paid a market value for their efforts, working for someone else.

During the time that they:
- poured their emotions into the business;
- put money into the business;
- invested emotional and physical energy into the business;
- sacrificed family time; and
- sacrificed personal time, hobbies, and friendships;

they were actually also making themselves worse off financially than if they had never started the business in the first place.

To Avoid That You Need To Get A Clear Picture

To avoid falling into the trap of being a Taker and suffering financial results below what you want and deserve you must first clearly define your Dream Lifestyle.

The first step in creating changes in your business so it starts moving toward supporting your Dream Lifestyle is to clearly **DEFINE** it. That will provide you with your target to make sure you don't stray off track, or settle for anything less.

To help you do that, I've included a process and worksheets that have been used by hundreds of business owners to work toward creating a crystal clear definition that they can act upon.

The exercises may seem simple. You may already have goals set for yourself. But you will find a lot of value in doing the following exercises anyway. They help you define your Dream Lifestyle in a very specific way that is very effective for you as a business owner.

Dream Lifestyle Exercise - Part One

In the space below write out a paragraph that describes your Dream Lifestyle. Describe how you would live your days, what kind of activities you would do, who you would do them with, when you would do them, and how you would feel about doing them. Include as many specific details as possible.

Include things such as:
- How would you wake up in the morning (happy and relaxed, for example)?
- What would you do after waking up, and before going into your business?
- Would you even go into your business? (some people want to build a business that runs without them even being there)
- When would you go in to the business?
- How would you get to your business (in a nice car, for example?)?
- How would your business "feel" when you walked in?
- How many people would be working in your business?
- How would your business look when you walked in?
- How would it smell?
- What would your office and desk look like?
- What would you do in the business?
- What would others do in the business?
- When would you leave for the day?
- What kind of mood would you be in when you left? (happy, relaxed, contented, etc)
- What would you do once you left the business for the day?
- What would you do in the evening of that day?
- Any other specific details you can add…

Description Of My Dream Lifestyle

Dream Lifestyle Exercise - Part Two

Re-read the elements you wrote down in Part One. For each of the elements from Part One, write down the REASON those things are important to you.

List each of these elements of your Dream Lifestyle below:

Element From Part 1	Why Important?

Chapter 3 – The Found Money Wheel

Now you understand that the true purpose of your business is to make money – enough money to fund your Dream Lifestyle. And you've gone through the process of clearly defining what your Dream Lifestyle looks like.

The reality, however, is that most businesses need some time to start creating the financial results that support the owner's Dream Lifestyle.

The reason it takes some time is that your business must use the money it generates to do other things BEFORE it can serve your Dream Lifestyle.

While the goal is to get your business to fund your Dream Lifestyle, doing that is only ONE of four things that your business needs to do with the money it creates.

And your business needs to do these other three things before it can fully support your Dream Lifestyle.

You need to be absolutely clear about what the four things are that your business needs to do with the money it creates. That's the only way you can truly understand the whole picture, do what needs to be done, and get to funding your Dream Lifestyle as quickly as possible.

The Four Things...

The four things your business does with the money it creates are:

1. **Repay Debts**
   This is the first use of the money your business creates. It's first because it is absolutely essential. Without doing this you won't be able to fully focus on the other uses of the money your business creates.

   If your business doesn't create enough money to support and repay its debts you will continually be distracted. You will waste physical and emotional resources fighting fires, solving the same problems over and over again, worrying about just surviving, and eroding your personal, emotional, and relationship energy and equity.

2. **Sustain Operations**
   This is the next most important use of the money your business creates. Being able to pay for your existing operations is a prerequisite to being able to generate more money to grow your business and fund your Dream Lifestyle.

   If your business does not create enough money to sustain operations you are forced to rely on cash that has already been built up, debt financing, or your personal cash resources. Each of these sources of cash decreases your net worth or equity, and increases your risk each time you are forced to rely on them.

3. **Re-Invest In Growth**
   This is where you can really start to drive your business forward so it starts creating financial results that serve your Dream Lifestyle.

   In order to generate enough money to fund your Dream Lifestyle you will probably find it necessary for your business to grow.

   The growth needed may be:
   - Growth in size (serving more customers – of the right type);
   - Growth in scale (adding more locations or expanding your current location);
   - Growth in your team (adding more team members – perhaps to allow you to focus on other areas of your business);
   - Growth in operations;
   - Growth in capacity; or
   - Any other number of areas.

   Growth is always easier and less risky, when it can be funded with money generated by your business rather than relying on debt, savings, or other outside sources.

   The reason you can do that with more ease and less risk is that when your business can create enough money to grow it becomes a renewable resource. If you make a mistake and it costs you some money you have the luxury of replacing that money with new money earned by your business.

   It's as close as you can get to having a "money tree" to support growth and your Dream Lifestyle.

4. **Fund Your Dream Lifestyle**
   This is the final use of the money your business generates.

   Dream Lifestyle does not simply refer to a life of "fast cars, yachts, and mansions". It certainly can mean those things, if that's truly the Dream Lifestyle you want. In reality, however, most truly successful business people also include non-material things in their Dream Lifestyles as well.

   It is the non-material things that most often give business owners their true passion and drive. Things that are made possible by money created by the business, but that benefit people other than the business owner directly.

   Common examples are helping out people who are less fortunate, contributing to church organizations or charities, or just being willing and able to do work for customers and clients who truly can't afford regular prices but are still worthy of help in the owners eyes.

   No matter what it is that makes up the definition of your Dream Lifestyle, you cannot fully realize it until your business first generates enough money to do the first three things.

Have You Ever Had a Flat Tire?

Now that you know the four uses of the money created by your business, how do you incorporate them into a practical model to help you achieve your desired financial outcome? How can you know where to focus your attention and energy at any one time?

A very effective way to do that is to envision a wheel.

If a wheel is nice and round it is a very efficient and effective method of moving a load from one place to another. It takes much less effort than carrying the load and enables a person to move the load much further with the same amount of effort.

But what happens if the wheel is not round? What if it is kind of lopsided – like when a tire on your car is flat?

With a flat tire, it is still possible to get the same load moved.

But the effort required to do that is much higher than when the wheel is nice and round. And if you move the load when the tire is too flat you actually end up causing damage to your vehicle and impair its ability to continue to move loads in the future.

In cases where your wheel loses air slowly the situation is more insidious. You end up exerting a small amount of extra effort each time your wheel loses a bit more air. Yu end up exerting a lot more effort over time but you don't even realize it is happening.

So you work harder to get the same results. And you don't even notice it until it's too late.

That is EXACTLY the situation the overwhelming majority of small business owners are in today. They are working way harder than they have to in order to get the results they are getting.

The physical limit on the amount of effort a business owner can exert over time automatically applies a limit on the financial results they can create.

To allow your business to create the financial results it needs to create in order to fulfill your Dream Lifestyle you need to make sure the "wheel" of your business is nice and round.

The Found Money Wheel Can Help

If you think about each of the four uses of the money your business creates as spokes on a wheel you get something called the Found Money Wheel. It is a nice visual way to envision all four things at the same time, and to assess how well your business is currently doing in each of these four areas.

The Found Money Wheel

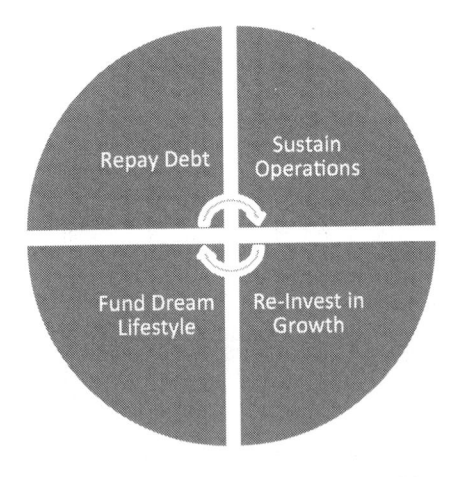

Repay Debt	Sustain Operations
Fund Dream Lifestyle	Re-Invest in Growth

This visual representation clearly shows that if too much focus is given to one of the four elements and the other areas are not given enough attention the "wheel" becomes unbalanced.

The unbalanced state of your Found Money Wheel makes it much, much more difficult to move your business toward creating the financial results you want from it. It will demand much more effort and resources than necessary to achieve **any** particular financial result.

Even a **poor** result will be a lot of hard work when your wheel is not balanced and round. If your business isn't allowing you to provide enough attention to each area of your business it won't be sustainable over time.

Creating Your Found Money Wheel

The way you create the Found Money Wheel for your business is to compare how well you feel your business is ***actually covering*** the amount it ***should be covering*** in each of the four areas.

For example, if you feel that your business has the following "coverage ratios" for each area:

- Repaying debts – 100% of its obligations are being funded;
- Sustaining existing operations – 100% of its obligations are being funded;
- Re-investing in growth – here you feel the business is only funding 25% of what it should be in its ideal state;
- Funding Dream Lifestyle – here you feel your business falls way short, and only funds 10% of what you would like it to fund.

Given this scenario, we know that the business and its owner will suffer over time. This business isn't sustainable, it isn't secure, and it will cause problems – now, soon, or down the road – unless things change.

There is a relatively small proportion of the money created going toward funding growth. It will therefore take longer to build up enough of a reserve to allow new things to be safely attempted or for new growth opportunities to be leveraged.

Most business owners find it necessary to grow the business, at least to some degree, in order to fund and serve their Dream Lifestyle. In this example, we know this to be true because the business is only providing 10% of what the owner defines as their Dream Lifestyle.

Yet this business is only generating 25% of the funds needed to grow the business. That means the remaining 75% must come from either the owner or from some other external source.

Having to rely on outside sources of cash to fund the required growth dramatically increases the stress and risk faced by the owners.

The 10% Dream Lifestyle coverage of this business tells us that the owner isn't getting what they really want from the business. That means the business is consuming emotional and physical energy from the owner. And that isn't sustainable over time and will eventually extract a huge mental, physical, emotional, and relationship cost.

The Found Money Wheel for the company in this example would look like this:

Found Money Wheel

Repay Debts

Fund Dream Lifestyle

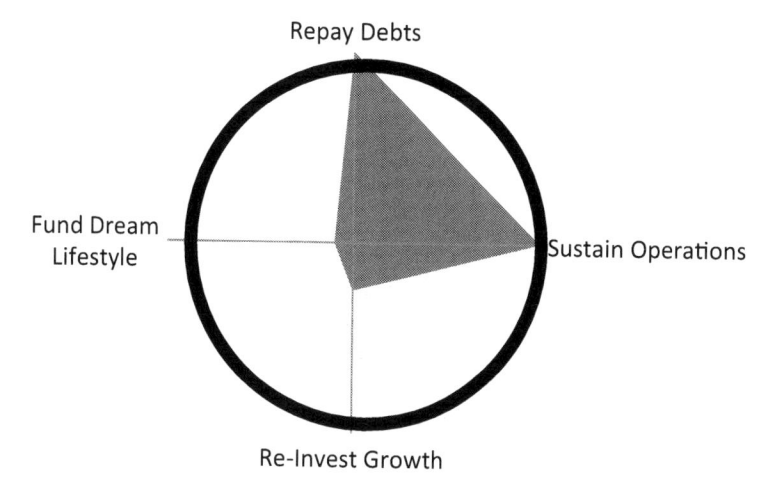

Sustain Operations

Re-Invest Growth

Clearly, this "wheel" is anything but round. And because it isn't round, like a real wheel, it is incredibly difficult to move the load the wheel is supposed to be carrying – in this case, carrying your business toward serving your Dream Lifestyle.

Life "Inside The Wheel"

This example demonstrates a Found Money Wheel for a typical small business.

The shape of this Found Money Wheel, coupled with 25 years of experience with thousands of businesses around the world allows the following description of "life inside" a business that has this particular shape of Found Money Wheel:

- The business most likely has a line of credit facility that is always, or almost always fully drawn, although the required payments are always made;

- The business has grown over the years and is often considered to be a "successful business" by customers, suppliers, and the business community;

- The business employs several people;

- The owner has some, or even many, of the outward trappings of a successful business (as commonly defined by others) – a large house, newer vehicles, golf memberships, investments, etc.

- The owner works a ton in the business and can never quite seem to be able to "afford" to hire that special person that would help free them up so they could enjoy some time away from the business.

What Does YOUR Found Money Wheel Look Like?

Creating your own Found Money Wheel will give you a lot of clarity around this concept and how it relates to you and your business.

For each statement below, select a response between 1 and 6 that reflects how well you believe the statement reflects your business in its current state. A score of "1" means that the statement absolutely does not apply, or is completely incorrect. A score of "6" means that the statement completely describes your business or is a completely true statement.

Statement	Agreement (scale of 1 – 6)
Our bills are always paid on time, each month.	6
When it comes time to make loan or credit card payments, we always make our payments on time.	6
Where possible, we take advantage of opportunities to pay down loans and credit cards quicker than the minimum requirement.	6
Overall, I am confident with the ability of my business to create enough money to make loan repayments and never worry about it.	3
When presented, there is always enough money in the business to take advantage of special pricing offers, or bulk purchases.	4
The business creates enough money that I can take advantage of opportunities to hire excellent team members when I get the chance.	2
There is always enough money in the bank account so that I never worry about making payroll or being able to pay my suppliers when amounts are due.	5
We always have enough of a "cash cushion" so we are never really panicked when an unexpected expense or repair arises.	4
I have set aside a "war chest" that allows me to take advantage of growth opportunities when they arise (i.e. new space, buying out competitors, etc).	2
My business creates enough money so I can hire high level team members that will allow me to focus on growth initiatives for the business.	~~2~~ 3
My business creates enough money so I can comfortably try new things and take calculated risks without risking the ability of my business to continue operating.	3
I feel that my business is providing enough money so I can afford to hire people to do the work that I	3

don't like to do so I can focus on areas in which I excel.	
My business provides enough money so that I can indulge in hobbies or interests outside of the business that I am passionate about.	2
I feel that my business serves me and allows me to fully realize my Dream Lifestyle.	2
My business allows me fulfill my "generosity desires" such as charitable giving, contributing to my church, etc.	2
I can always take the time I want away from my business without worrying about it or feeling out of control.	5

Then take the average score for the questions indicated and then plot them on the blank chart that follows:

Questions		Element
1 – 4	5.25	Repay Debts
5 – 8	3.75	Sustain Operations
9 – 12	2.75	Re-Invest in Growth
13 – 16	2.75	Fund Dream Lifestyle

Connect them with a line for a better visual of the shape of your Found Money Wheel. There's a blank template on the next page to help you with this.

Your Found Money Wheel
Date: _____

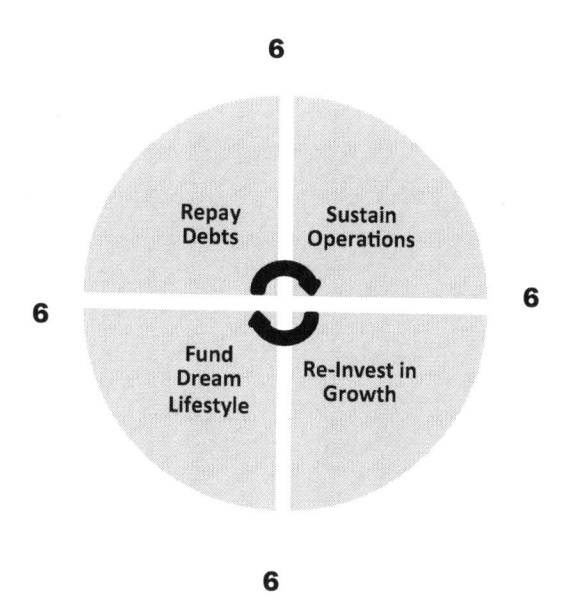

6

Repay Debts	Sustain Operations
Fund Dream Lifestyle	Re-Invest in Growth

6   6

6

Chapter 4 – When Does Your Business Actually Make Money?

That's really THE question for you and your business.

After all, at the end of each day, week, month, and year, if it's to be successful, your business MUST make money. It needs to make money so it can repay debt, sustain its operations, re-invest in growth, and fund your Dream Lifestyle.

The sad news is that most small businesses don't make enough money to do all of those things. The place almost every small business falls short is in the area of funding Dream Lifestyle. Most small business owners simply haven't created a business that creates enough money to fulfill their Dream Lifestyle – instead their business seems to **juuuusssssst** make enough to let them **get by**.

And sadly, many small businesses also fall short in the area of creating enough money to re-invest in growth. That means that they are unable to take advantage of opportunities that could increase the financial results the business generates. There is a reason for the old saying, "the rich get richer".

The reason is that it's accurate.

If you have money, you can take advantage of opportunities to re-invest in growth and make even more money.

In the current economic environment, many businesses even fall short in the "sustaining operations" category. That situation requires additional cash injections. These cash injections come from outside lenders which can be challenging to get. Or the funds must come from your personal savings or equity which exposes you to increased risk and stress.

At the end of the day, the harsh truth is that if your business isn't making enough money to fulfill all four of those elements of success (repay debt, sustain operations, re-invest in growth, and fund your Dream Lifestyle) – it is failing.

It's failing because it isn't sustainable over the long term if it can't generate enough money to do ALL four of those things. And if it isn't sustainable over the long term then it is in the process of failing and it is only a matter of time before it stops operating (either out of necessity, or because you are unable to take the emotional and physical toll anymore).

If you are thinking, "Hey, my business isn't currently doing all four of those things", I've got two things to tell you:

1. You are just like the vast majority of other small business owners in the world today – because most of them feel exactly the same way; and

2. Don't get discouraged. Because it doesn't have to stay that way (and certainly won't stay that way if you apply what you learn in this book)

You can change your fear into confidence and action. You can start driving your business toward making more money – toward making enough money to accomplish those four things.

You just have to follow the process and commit to taking action.

It Starts With Knowing How

The critical key to success here is for you to know *how your business makes money*. Once you know that, and understand it, you can start making decisions to control both *how* your business makes money, and *how much* it makes.

You will have an almost unlimited range of options for creating a business to serve your Dream Lifestyle.

Right now, however, if you're like about 95% of the small business owners out there, you aren't really sure how your business creates the financial results it creates. And because of that you feel adrift when it comes to your financial results.

You hope for the best; rely on luck, the economy and your competitors; and are always a little bit tentative when making business decisions because you're not sure what the financial impact will be.

So How DOES Your Business Make Money?

Ahhhhh, now we're into the "million dollar" question.

After all, you need to know HOW it makes money so you can get CONTROL over the PROCESS of creating the financial results you want.

For your business to make money it must do three things. *And it must do them all at the same time.*

To make money your business must:
- Generate a positive net profit; and
- Give you an adequate return on investment; and
- Generate a strong enough positive cash flow

We'll cover each of these three things in more detail in a moment. But for now, I want you to get used to thinking about your business doing all three of these things, and doing them all at the same time.

Too often business owners fall into the trap of thinking their business only needs to do ONE of these three things for it to make money. It's like they become mesmerized into thinking they can pick one the three elements, focus their attention on it, and things will be great.

For example, they may focus only on net profit, and lose sight of the importance of generating an adequate return on investment, or positive cash flow. That myopic view can lead to situations where they pursue growth, chase new markets, or seek additional revenue when those things might just be the absolute WORST things to do!

Or sometimes owners focus too much on the cash flow of their business. They fall into the trap of thinking that if there's cash in their bank, and more of it coming in, then things are rolling right along. That can lead to situations where they pursue growth opportunities when they really shouldn't be.

The result is often a devastating cash crunch when the owner is blind-sided by something they didn't expect (but should have).

You may have fallen victim to one of those traps in your business. In fact, you probably have. But don't worry. You won't be making those mistakes any longer.

Triple-Overlap – Your Key To A Money-Making Business

A great way to think about these three elements (net profit, return on investment and cash flow) is to picture three overlapping circles.

The area where they overlap is the <u>only place</u> your business will actually make money for you. It looks like the diagram on the following page:

The Found Money Triple Overlap

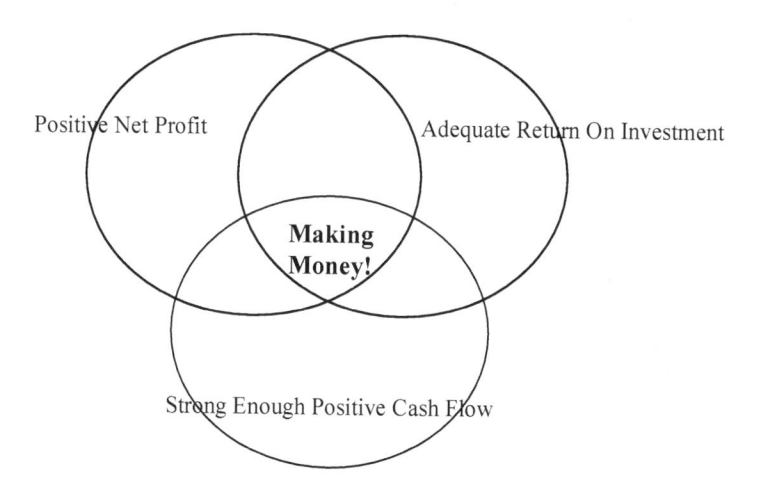

Positive Net Profit

Adequate Return On Investment

Making Money!

Strong Enough Positive Cash Flow

Your goal as a business owner is to constantly pay attention to *all three* elements of making money – positive net profit, adequate return on investment, and positive cash flow – *at all times*. You must manage your business to create a Triple Overlap. And make it as large as possible (because that's when it makes you the most money).

Watch Out For The Danger Zones

The areas that are inside any one of the circles (or even inside two of the circles), but that are not inside the "triple-overlap" area are what we call "danger zones". They tend to trick business owners and draw them into a dangerous trap.

They may look appealing, and you might be tempted to focus solely on one of them, but please don't.

How can they be Danger Zones when they are each part of making money? How can positive net profit be dangerous?

Good questions.

And in actual fact, each element, itself, isn't dangerous. I call them Danger Zones because they have the potential to trick you into ignoring the true Triple Overlap. They can take you into areas that can cause very unpleasant consequences. They can seduce you into thinking they are "just what you're looking for".

They can fool you into focusing on just one of the elements and thinking that "everything is just fine." And if that happens, you will likely end up like the naked emperor in the classic fairy tale who thought everything was fine when it was clear that it wasn't. Only you might just lose your business and your wealth, instead of "just" your clothes.

Over the years, I've come across thousands of small business owners who fell into this trap.

For example, they would focus almost exclusively on sales in an effort to increase net profit. Their mistaken belief was that if they could increase their sales, they would automatically increase net profit and would make more money.

But often the increase in net profit comes at the expense of maintaining good cash flow and the business owners ends up with LESS money than before – even though they have MORE net profit.

Sound familiar to you?

It might – because most business owners fall into that trap at some point in their business career. The lucky ones survive it and learn to look at their Triple Overlap.

The same trap applies to the other Danger Zones. After all, if a business is making a healthy net profit, it's easy to assume that all is going well. If a business has a strong cash flow, it's easy to assume that things are great. The danger, however, is that those assumptions are dead wrong.

And they are often hiding a disaster about to happen.

What Is Net Profit?

There are a lot of accounting books out there that give some "very nice" definitions of net profit. They provide "nice" long, detailed descriptions of the various types of expenses, a bit about their history, and so on.

That type of discussion about net profit is, however, is REEEAAALLY boring. Even to people who are trained accountants, like me.

The good news is that to improve your financial results you don't need to worry about that level of detailed knowledge. If you want to learn those boring details, and kill your chances of being the center of attention at parties (a little accounting humor, there) go ahead.

We're not going to be doing that here, though. Instead, we're going to define net profit in a very practical and usable way.

Ready for it?

Here it is – net profit is simply the "thing" that's left over after all the expenses your business generates are subtracted from all the revenue it creates.

Read that paragraph again. Actually, to make sure you do, here it is again:

Net profit is the thing that's left over after you gather up all the expenses your business generates, and subtract them from all the revenue it creates.

The most important part of that definition for you to <u>understand</u> is the phrase, *"left over"*.

You see, an awful lot of business owners "know" the definition of net profit. You probably "know" it as well – intuitively that is. You *know* that it's what remains after all your expenses are subtracted from your revenues.

What Is Cash Flow?

Cash flow is simply ALL the cash that comes *into* your business, less ALL the cash that flows *out of* your business. Think of it like the ocean tide. It sweeps into your business, and then sweeps out again. It ebbs and flows in a continual and endless cycle.

And while it ebbs and flows, you must use your good business skills and management to ensure not all of the cash that sweeps into your business sweeps back out. You need to make sure that some (more is always better) cash stays behind with each cycle.

Common sources of cash inflows in your business are:
- Cash sales
- Collecting accounts receivable
- Cash from borrowing
- Cash you have injected into your business
- Cash from selling a piece of equipment or other assets
- Cash invested by owners (good old you)

Common sources of cash outflows are:
- The payment of wages and other operating expenses
- Repayments made on loans
- Payments to shareholders and owners
- Paying accounts payable
- Purchasing new equipment or other assets

What Cash Flow Is NOT

It is critical that you are totally clear about something. Please pay attention because it sure does trip up a lot of business owners. This thing is…….

CASH FLOW IS NOT NET PROFIT!

Cash flow is a critical element of the Triple Overlap required for your business to make you money.

Cash flow is what actually gives *you* the resources to expand your business, hire more team members so you can pursue other interests and live your life at a higher level.

Cash flow makes it possible for your business to function. It's a simple fact that you can't "spend" net profits or assets. All you can "spend" is cash.

If you don't believe that, next time you're trying to buy a candy bar, simply bring out your financial statements and tell the clerk that your business made money, and you'll give them $1 of that profit for the candy bar, then walk out.

See how far you get before the police arrive and grab you for shoplifting (don't really try it, naturally, but I think you get my point).

Calculating Cash Flow From Your Business:

Here's the "formula" for calculating the cash flow generated by your business. Don't be intimidated - just follow it through and it will work out.

Cash Flow Formula

	Net profit from business
+	Accounts Receivable at *start*
-	Accounts Receivable at *end*
+	Inventory at *start*
-	Inventory at *end*
+	Accounts Payable at *end*
-	Accounts Payable at *start*
+	Cash from assets *sold*
-	Cash paid to *purchase* new assets
+	Depreciation / Amortization
-	Debt at *start*
+	Debt at *end*
	Cash Flow!!!!!!

A closer look at this formula shows why it's possible for your business to earn a great net profit, and still be starved for cash.

The reason is that when it comes to cash flow net profit is only the *starting point* for cash flow. There are an awful lot of things that happen to net profit as it travels down the formula and turns into cash flow.

There is certainly a relationship between cash flow and net profit, but it's an indirect connection. That fact often trips up a lot of small business owners. That's the reason you need to pay attention to cash flow in addition to net income.

Not paying attention to the cash flow formula, by the way, is a very common habit (a bad habit) for legions of small business owners. This habit is usually caused by a failure to realize what exactly causes cash flow (the elements of this formula).

The great news is that this is usually a very "fixable" problem.

Poor, or negative, cash flow can be stopped and improved easily and quickly. It becomes a matter of looking at changes in the components of the cash flow formula to determine where cash is being "sucked up".

What is Return on Investment?

Return on Investment (ROI) is a measure that "tells you" is just how effectively your business converts money into more money.

It is really just a measure of how efficient your business is. Just like an automobile that has a fuel efficiency rating in terms of "miles per gallon", ROI measures the "money out per money in" for your business.

ROI is actually quite an intuitive concept that we use almost daily in many areas of our lives. For example, financial institutions scream about the rate of interest they will pay us for our deposits. All else being equal, it's only natural you would deposit your money with the one that's going to give the highest rate of interest (the highest return on your investment).

Similarly, when we consider taking a new job, we weigh the benefits the new job will create compared to the "things" that will be given up by leaving the old job – and obviously the more "new benefits" that are gained compared to the "old benefits" given up, the more attractive the new opportunity is.

Clearly the logic behind measuring ROI is obvious and simple.

But, strangely, when it comes to running a business, this intuitive concept often gets completely ignored (or forgotten) by an awful lot of business owners. And the odds are high that you're one of them. But don't worry. Because from now on YOU are going to be one of the successful business owners that considers ROI and harnesses its power to create the business you want.

A Deeper Look At ROI

Before we go any further with our discussion about measuring, managing, and controlling ROI we need to take a look at what ROI actually means.
- "Return" refers to the net profit your business creates;
- "Investment" refers to the amount of money you've got tied up (invested in) your business.

What Kind of Assets Are We Talking About?

The way we are going to look at assets when we're talking about ROI is different from the traditional "accounting" view of assets. Don't worry about trying to win any arguments with accounting purists – we just want to understand how to make money in your business.

Assets are simply anything that your business owns. That means assets can include everything from cash to accounts receivable, to inventory (and yes, even service professionals have inventory as you will soon see), to equipment and other capital assets that have been acquired over the years.

But we can't just look at all your assets, because remember, what we are trying to measure is the cash that you have invested in your business. Cash is represented by actual bank balances (naturally), as well as all your other assets (like those listed above).

But we also need to account for the fact that not all of your assets have been "purchased" with cash. There is almost always some type of financing involved. It may be long-term loans for equipment or other capital assets, it can be bank overdrafts or lines of credit, and it can be vendor financing in the form of accounts payable.

So to get to the number that truly represents the amount of money you have invested in your business, you will need to somehow subtract the "financing portion" of your business from your total assets.

Sounds a little tricky, doesn't it?

But you are in luck.

Because there is actually a really simple and easy way to get the number you will need. The number you need is called "equity" on your financial statements.

With one little modification.

If you are a service business, you will need to modify the equity from your tax return or financial statements to account for your inventory. That is because, with the exception of law firms, accounting firms, and similar professional firms, service businesses often do not track their inventory.

Before you think that doesn't apply to your business, you need to know something…

Yes, YOUR Business DOES Have Inventory!

Inventory refers to all the assets you've accumulated in your business that you intend to sell to your customers or clients. Inventory is obvious in a retail or manufacturing type of business where something is made, or purchased, to be re-sold.

But what's not so obvious is what I call "hidden inventory". Hidden inventory exists in EVERY business.

For the purpose of managing your business, you need to consider inventory to be ANY investment you've made into something you expect to sell to a customer. Our broader definition of inventory (compared to the accounting definition) explains why many businesses run into problems when they don't expect it and certainly don't see the problem coming.

Here's a real life example to illustrate how broad this definition is, and why it matters to you.

Once I was called to come visit and consult with the business owner of a busy flooring company. They sold carpet, hardwood, tile, laminate, and all other types of flooring.

The call from the owner was prompted by his frustration over being so busy in his company, having a steady stream of customers (both retail and through insurance companies), a great brand and market reputation, yet struggling to create financial performance that produced the cash he was expecting.

While analyzing his business from a Found Money perspective, I began mapping out his business process flows to look for "hidden inventory" and areas where there was a build up of investment in his business.

As I was spending the first hour having him tour me through his store, highlighting his operation and workflow, I was struck by a large amount of papers at an official-looking desk in the corner of the sales floor.

Enquiring about it, I was told that it was the desk of the lady who managed the sales for the company. He proudly showed me the stack of forms where she had prepared quotations for customers after they had come into the store, consulted with her, made selections of products, and then asked for a quote.

Sounds like a good thing to be that busy, right?

The problem was that when I asked to do an analysis of the stack of quotes (I geek out when I'm working with a client and there isn't a stone that doesn't go unturned), I discovered two things.

The first was that a lot of the quotes had dates going back a couple of weeks. The second thing I discovered was that the "client copy" was still attached to each quote.

What I discovered was that the business owner's sales person was someone he took tremendous pride in keeping super busy and running a "lean" operation.

The problem was that she was so busy working with customers who came in to the busy store that she wasn't actually getting quotes out to the customers so sales were not closing as fast as they should have been.

The fix was easy, but counterintuitive.

Hire an assistant for this salesperson (adding more cost to the operation) in order to free up time so quotes could be prepared and sent out the same day a customer asked for them. This would pull sales forward faster and overall accelerate the cash flow cycle – from customer initiation to check being received.

The ROI Formula

The formula used by the Found Money system for ROI is as follows:

$$\text{Return on Investment} = \frac{\text{Net Profit}}{\text{Net Assets (equity + untracked inventory)}}$$

ROI measures how much you get out of your business (net profit) compared to how much you put into it (investment in assets). It makes sense, then, that having an ROI that increases over time is a great thing.

Your goal should be to maximize resources – and the more profit you can get for a given amount of assets the better it is for you, your business, and your employees.

This brings us to the Found Money Rule of ROI:

Your business cannot make money for you if your investment in assets increases at a faster rate than your net profit.

If this rule gets violated, as it so often does, you simply won't see much money from your business.

Putting Yourself Into The ROI Equation

When it comes to thinking of inventory in your business, pay particularly close attention to YOUR time as an owner.

Experience with hundreds of business owners around the world has shown over and over again that generally, owners give away way too much of their time without considering the financial impact that has.

Value your time, and track it to get a true picture of the ROI your business creates for you.

Think about it this way. Suppose your Dream Lifestyle has you earning $100,000 per year, and working 3 days per week with 6 weeks of vacation each year.

That translates into about 126 working days for you each year. If we assume as well that your Dream Lifestyle involves you working no more than an 8 hour day, that means a total "work year" of 1,008 hours.

Doing the division you can calculate, therefore, that your business will need to earn you a little bit more than $99 for each hour you work.

In other words, you need to think of your time as being worth at least $99 per hour. That means that if your business isn't earning you the equivalent of $99 per hour, in this example, that you have "tied up" cash (in the form of opportunity cost relative to your Dream Lifestyle).

Let's look at an example to make this clear. Imagine you have a Dream Lifestyle definition that includes the information shown in the following table:

	Dream Lifestyle	Actual – Scenario 1	Actual – Scenario 2
Annual Income	$100,000	$75,000	$100,000
Annual Hours	1,008	2,000	2,150
Net / Hour	$99.20	$37.50	$46.50
Equity (from financials)	$15,000	$15,000	$15,000
Apparent ROI	667%	500%	667%
Additional "Inventory"	=(2,000 – 1,008)*($99.20 - $37.50)	$61,213	
Additional "Inventory"	=(2,150 – 1,008) * ($46.50 - 99.20)		$60,177
Revised Equity	$15,000	$76,213	$75,177
"True" ROI	667%	98%	133%

What this example shows is that, by not paying attention to your "inventory" in considering your ROI, you are literally making it impossible for you to get a clear picture and understanding of how much your business is giving you in return for your investment (of money and time).

Chapter 5 – Is YOUR Business Making Money?

Have you ever tried to find a specific location and called someone for directions?

Admit it.

We've all been there a "time or two" before. When you call the other person for directions, what's the first thing they ask you before giving you a single direction?

"Where are you right now?"

That question makes perfect sense. After all, if the other person isn't clear where you're starting from, their best intentions and most skillful directions will be completely useless to you. In fact those ill-considered directions could even be dangerous!

They need to understand where you are starting from if they are going to help you get where you want to go.

Your business is just like that.

You're going to be working hard to take your business somewhere new. Somewhere where it's in tune with your Dream Lifestyle, and where it becomes a vehicle for you to create the life you want.

But before you can decide what you need to do to "get there" you first have to figure out exactly where your business is starting from - right now. You must discover where your business is at in terms of your Triple Overlap – if it's actually making money for you. And if it isn't making money, where is the problem?

It doesn't matter what financial results your business has been creating up to this point in time. It simply doesn't matter *where* your business is right now. You can take control and start moving toward where you want it to be.

But what does matter is that you *know where you are starting from*. Only then can you create a useful roadmap to start moving your business to where you want it to be.

Is Your Business Making Money?

Let's get started figuring out where your business is starting from.

To do that you are going to examine the three most recent fiscal years your business has completed. If you prefer, or if it makes more sense for your business, you can choose the three most recent periods, other than fiscal years. For example, you might decide to use the three most recent quarters if your business is in its first year.

Then fill in the information for each of the three periods in the table on the next page.

Your Triple Overlap

Summary of "Triple Overlap" For _____

		Most Recent Year	Next Most Recent Year	Next Most Recent Year
A	Sales			
B	Net Profit			
C	Equity			
D	Cash Flow			
B/A x100	Net Profit (%)			
D/A x 100	Cash Flow (%)			
B/C x 100	ROI (%)			

On the next page you will find a *cash flow worksheet* to help you calculate your cash flow for each period. It looks a little more complicated, but don't let that panic you. Just follow along, and let the worksheet guide you through the process.

Cash Flow Calculation Worksheet

	Most Recent Year	Next Most Recent Year	Next Most Recent Year
Net Earnings			
Add A/R – start	+	+	+
Subtract A/R – end	−	−	−
Add Inventory – start	+	+	+
Subtract Inventory – end	−	−	−
Add A/P – end	+	+	+
Subtract A/P – start	−	−	−
Add Cash from assets sold	+	+	+
Subtract Cash to buy new equipment	−	−	−
Add Depreciation	+	+	+
Add Debt – end	+	+	+
Subtract Debt – start	−	−	−
Cash Flow			

The Found Money Chart – Visual Application of the Triple Overlap

The Triple Overlap is a great way to visualize the three things that must happen in order for your business to make money.

When it comes to actually calculating a Triple Overlap for your business, however, that nice little overlapping circle diagram isn't very "user friendly". As a result of that, and based on work with hundreds of small business owners we created a user-friendly tool.

It is called the Found Money Chart.

The Found Money Chart is a more effective way to analyze your current Triple Overlap and identify areas where you should focus at least some of your efforts in the near team.

To create your Found Money Chart you can follow the example below. The numbers of have been filled in to serve as an example of how the Found Money Chart works.

Year	Sales	Net Profit	Cash Flow	Equity
Year 1	$450,000	$115,000	$ 85,000	$300,000
Year 2	$375,000	$105,000	$ 95,000	$185,000
Year 3	$325,000	$ 95,000	$ 95,000	$ 80,000

The next step is to convert net profit to a percentage of sales, and cash flow to a percentage of sales. ROI will be calculated by converting net profit to a percentage of equity.

The table below shows the results of this calculation:

Year	Sales (%)	Net Profit (%)	Cash Flow (%)	ROI (%)
Year 1	100%	26%	19%	38%
Year 2	100%	28%	25%	57%
Year 3	100%	29%	29%	119%

Below is the resulting chart when the results of the table above are plotted. Doing this identifies any dangerous trends as well as makes it easier to see what decisions and actions are required to improve any negative trends.

Found Money Chart – From Sample Data Above

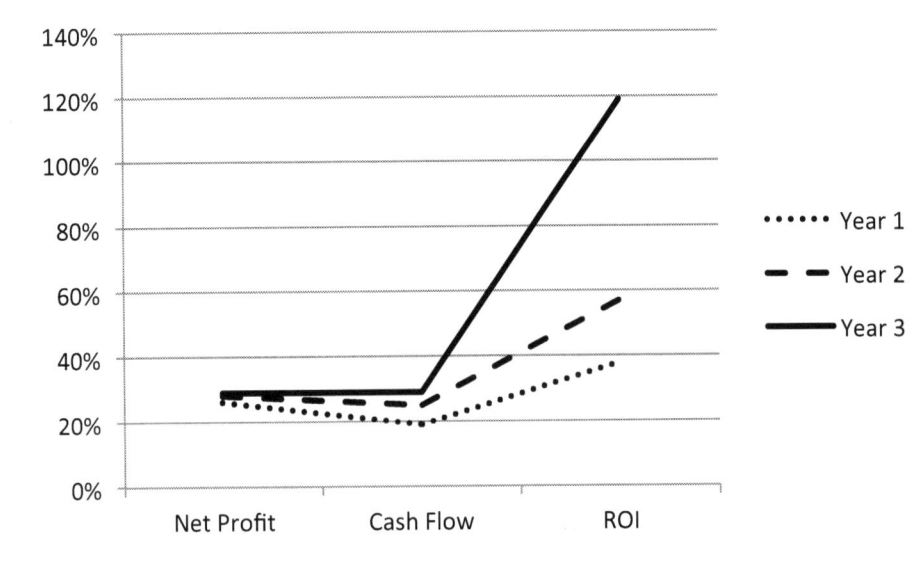

Analyzing the Found Money Chart

When you look at the Found Money Chart it becomes easy to spot trouble areas.

Looking at the Found Money Chart above, several things immediately jump out.

Net profit as a percentage of sales has been dropping in each of the last three years. This means that, even though sales have been increasing, the business has been "keeping" less and less of the increase in revenue. In other words, the business owner is working harder and harder to make less and less;

Cash flow as a percentage of sales has been less than net profit (as a percentage of sales) in the last two years. This means that the business has not been generating positive cash flow – and the owner, the bank, or both, have been forced to inject cash to continue sustaining operations. Furthermore, this cash shortfall means the business has not been able to re-invest in growth, and most certainly hasn't been funding the owner's Dream Lifestyle;

ROI has been dropping precipitously over the last three years. This highlights a likely trouble spot. It could be caused by the owner being forced to "remove" equity built up in the business to fund their lifestyle, or to generate cash.

Creating a Found Money Chart for your business gives you a visual representation of what you may have "felt" but been unable to pinpoint has been happening in your business.

So go ahead and do it for your business now. Then use your data and your Found Money Chart to identify trends and issues in the exercise that follows.

Your Turn – Is YOUR Business Making Money?

Now it's your turn to analyze your business. Let's take a look to see if it is making you money and analyze any trends in its Triple Overlap that require your attention.

Gather up the necessary information to complete the two tables below.

Enter the actual sales, net profit, cash flow (you may need to use the cash flow worksheet in the earlier module), and equity data for your business.

Found Money Chart Data Collection				
Year	**Sales**	**Net Profit**	**Cash Flow**	**Equity**

In the table below, convert the data above into percentages as shown in the example earlier. You can also use the Found Money Chart software template to do the calculations and simply enter them below.

Found Money Chart Data Collection				
Year	**Sales (%)**	**Net Profit (%)**	**Cash Flow (%)**	**Equity (%)**

Now plot your percentages for the last three periods to create your own Found Money Chart.

Identifying Your Found Money Chart Trends and Issues

You have now created your Found Money Chart and have taken the momentous step of discovering if your business is truly making you any money. The vast majority of small business owners out there never, ever do this and, therefore, they continue to operate blindly – relying on guesses, luck, and other outside forces.

In the space below, record your 4 most major trends or issues that you see when examining your Found Money Chart.

Found Money Chart Issue / Trend #1
_____
_____
_____
_____

Found Money Chart Issue / Trend #2
_____
_____
_____
_____

Found Money Chart Issue / Trend #3

_____
_____
_____
_____
_____

Found Money Chart Issue / Trend #4

_____
_____
_____
_____
_____

Chapter 6 – The PROCESS Of Net Profit

Net profit is the cornerstone of making money in your business. Of course your business must also generate cash flow and an adequate ROI at the same time. But net profit is where it all begins, and it is net profit that drives your financial results.

That means you must become a "net profit master".

You need to be able to understand how net profit is created in your business, as well as how to change and control the amount of net profit created.

When it comes to net profit, however, there is an interesting paradox that holds many business owners back. It can be summarized like this:

While creating net profit is critical to producing your financial results, by the time you know what your net profit is, **it is too late to do anything about it!**

In other words, it's simply *impossible* for you to do anything about net profit, other than measure it. Net profit, as a financial concept, is something that just happens. It's like yesterday's "high temperature" that always gets reported on The Weather Network.

The high temperature can't be determined until after the fact. It's interesting and useful, in some ways and you can make some guesses based on that information. But there's nothing you can do to change it.

So What Can You Do About Net Profit?

That poses a problem that causes most business owners to throw up their hands in frustration. And it's a problem that results in the way almost every small business owner operates – doing stuff; trying stuff; marketing blindly; and hoping that, somehow, an adequate net profit is going to result from all the "activity and action".

But that approach causes you, the business owner, to become a Taker. Helplessly doing what you hope will work, and then "going along for the ride" and hoping your business will allow you to "take" enough money.

But there is a way to avoid being a helpless Taker. A way to know what must be done, and what must happen in order to create the net profit you want so that your business serves your Dream Lifestyle.

The way to do that is to admit you can't "control" net profit, but realize that you *CAN* control the things that *create* net profit.

The creation of net profit in your business is a process – nothing more. The definition of a process is "a series of actions or operations conducing to an end" (www.merriam-webster.com). And that's exactly what net profit is – the culmination of a series of activities.

So there you have it. Net profit is nothing more than a process. And because it is a process, you can identify the specific activities and steps that create the end result.

And just like any other process, if you change (manage) the activities in the process, you alter (manage) the outcome.

The good news is that your business isn't really all that complex. It's not a nuclear reactor (unless your business happens to be nuclear reactors!). And that makes it a fairly basic task to identify, manage, control, and affect the activities that create revenue and expenses in your business.

That means it is fairly easy to control and direct the ***process*** of creating net profit.

Here is simple example to illustrate:

<u>Responding to Web Enquiries</u>
> We have all visited websites of businesses that we may be looking to engage or buy from. And we have all seen somewhere on the website where we can enter an enquiry about their products or services, or request more information.
>
> The way your business responds to these types of requests and the actions it takes is a key activity in the process of creating net profit.
>
> It may seem a little bit mundane but it's probably one of the most crucial factors in the process of creating net profit.
>
> Replying to a web enquiry or to a request for more information is usually the first contact a client or prospect has with your business. And how that activity gets performed has a huge impact on the quantity and quality of customers your business attracts.
>
> So if you and your team work to come up with a better and more effective way of responding to web enquiries in a quick, impressive, and helpful way, the activity of

responding to web enquiries can create more revenue, reduce the time of your average sales cycle, and even reduce costs.

The activity of responding to web enquiries affects revenue and expenses, and therefore affects your net profit. But it's only by impacting or altering the activity that you can actually **impact** the result (net profit).

A diagram of the activity in this example might look like this:

Respond to Enquiry → Create Revenue → Create Expenses → Net Profit

Notice how it's the activity of responding to web enquiries that is the key to creating the revenue and expenses. It's the ACTIVITY that ultimately affects net profit.

Getting Customers To Buy More

Another activity that can really boost the process of creating net profit is to invite your customers to buy more from you when it makes sense given their needs.

Here's an example from a recent experience I had with the popular CRM app, Salesforce.com.

I was doing some work for a company that uses Salesforce and we had been working on changing some of their processes and workflows in its Salesforce instance.

About two days after making a specific group of changes, I received an email and then a phone call from an account rep saying "I noticed your sales team has been creating a lot of quotes in Salesforce. As your business continues to grow, is this functionality keeping up with how quickly your team is selling? "

Then she went on to let me know that Salesforce had an additional product that had a track record of reducing quote turnaround times by 80%.

That level of attention is impressive isn't it?

By being aware of their customers and the potential need for additional features, Salesforce was able to offer something that made their product even more valuable.

And at the same time increasing their financial performance. A win for both of us!

In other words, by doing a specific set of activities (identify a potential unfulfilled need of an existing customer and reaching out to that customer), Salesforce.com is increasing their net profit and overall financial performance.

These are just two examples to prime your "mental pump".

They are meant to show you how you can manage and control the activities that are part of the process of net profit. But remember, you can't directly manage and control net profit. So stop thinking about net profit as something you can control or manage. You can't. So stop trying.

Start thinking of net profit as the logical outcome of a series of activities (a process). With that perspective you CAN control the activities in the process. And that's how you can manage, change, and create the net profit you want from your business.

Mapping Your Process of Net Profit

Since net profit is a process, and that means you can control, direct and manage it, it's time to look at how you can do that.

The easiest way to accomplish that is to view the process of creating net profit like this:

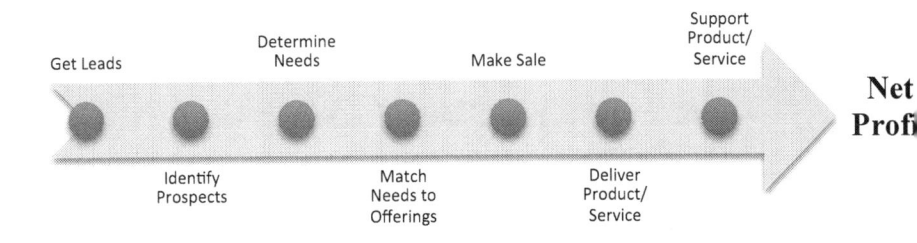

Get Leads → Identify Prospects → Determine Needs → Match Needs to Offerings → Make Sale → Deliver Product/Service → Support Product/Service → Net Profit

The process of creating net profit, when visualized in this manner becomes a matter of executing several steps, over and over again. This breaks the process down into smaller "chunks" that are easier to focus on. The sum of all these "parts" is your net profit.

Exercise - Mapping Your Process of Net Profit

Using the diagram above, and your knowledge of how your business currently operates, it is now time to think about the elements that form the process of net profit in your business.

Below you will find separate sections for each of the steps in creating the net profit your business generates. For each section, list as many activities that are done in your business for that step in the net profit process.

For some steps, you may have very few activities listed. That is entirely possible because each business has a unique model for creating net profit.

Your focus in doing this exercise should be on listing / identifying the activities that actually are done. Use caution to avoid listing activities you THINK happen or that you think SHOULD happen. Be honest with yourself and list only those activities that actually occur.

List as much detail / as many activities as possible. Even if it seems "minor" take the time to list it – often it is though "minor" activities that mean the most when identifying your process of net profit.

The activities that we do to GENERATE LEADS are:

_____
_____
_____
_____
_____
_____
_____
_____

Ways we can improve our activities to GENERATE Leads are:

_____
_____
_____
_____
_____
_____
_____
_____

The activities that we do to IDENTIFY PROSPECTS are:

_____
_____
_____
_____
_____
_____
_____
_____
_____
_____

Ways we can improve our activities to IDENTIFY PROSPECTS are:

_____
_____
_____
_____
_____
_____
_____
_____
_____
_____

The activities that we do to DETERMINE NEEDS are:

_____
_____
_____
_____
_____
_____
_____
_____
_____

Ways we can improve our activities to DETERMINE NEEDS are:

_____
_____
_____
_____
_____
_____
_____
_____
_____
_____

The activities that we do to MATCH NEEDS TO PRODUCTS / SERVICES are:

_____
_____
_____
_____
_____
_____
_____
_____
_____

Ways we can improve our activities to MATCH NEEDS TO PRODUCTS / SERVICES are:

_____
_____
_____
_____
_____
_____
_____
_____
_____
_____

The activities that we do to MAKE THE SALE are:

_____
_____
_____
_____
_____
_____
_____
_____
_____
_____

Ways we can improve our activities to MAKE THE SALE are:

_____
_____
_____
_____
_____
_____
_____
_____
_____
_____

The activities that we do to DELIVER PRODUCTS / SERVICES are:

_____
_____
_____
_____
_____
_____
_____
_____
_____
_____

Ways we can improve our activities to DELIVER PRODUCTS / SERVICES are:

_____
_____
_____
_____
_____
_____
_____
_____
_____
_____

The activities that we do to SUPPORT PRODUCTS / SERVICES are:

_____
_____
_____
_____
_____
_____
_____
_____

Ways we can improve our activities to SUPPORT PRODUCTS / SERVICES are:

_____
_____
_____
_____
_____
_____
_____
_____

Chapter 7 – Gross Profit 101

The concept of gross profit is poorly understood by most small business owners. I believe the reason is that gross profit has been traditionally treated as a "cost accounting" concept. And it has been made needlessly complex and downright boring by traditional accounting.

The concept, however, rather than being merely a "cost accounting" concept, is actually very important when it comes to creating specific financial results.

Once you understand what gross profit is, you can start using it to drive the financial results your business creates.

Why Is Gross Profit So Important?

The simple answer to that question is that Gross Profit is the "thing" that allows your business to cover your overhead, repay loans, provide money to re-invest in growth, and fund your Dream Lifestyle.

And (hopefully) you remember from earlier lessons that the four things just mentioned above are also the four things your business MUST do if it is to be successful.

So, in other words, Gross Profit is the "engine" that makes it possible for your business to make money, and be sustainable over the long-term. Without Gross Profit, your business will simply die. Sooner (usually) or later.

Gross Profit In Action

Let's look at some examples of why Gross Profit is so important to your business.

Assume your business has sales revenue of $150,000, and direct costs totaling $55,000. That would mean that your business had a gross profit of $95,000 (sales revenue of $150,000 less direct costs of $55,000).

In other words, after creating $150,000 in revenue, and paying the costs directly attributable to those sales ($55,000) you would have $95,000 "left over" to cover your overhead, re-invest in growth, repay debts, and fund your Dream Lifestyle.

Of course, this assumption only holds if you have paid attention to your Triple Overlap and maintained positive cash flow (i.e. haven't "bought" sales revenue by allowing customers to run balances with you).

Now suppose you have overhead of $45,000.

A summary of your financial results is shown below:

Sales Revenue	$150,000
Direct Costs	$ 55,000
Gross Profit	$ 95,000 (63.3%)
Overhead	$ 45,000
Net Profit	**$ 50,000**

(to fund repay debt, re-invest in growth, fund Dream Lifestyle)

If out of your $50,000 net profit you had to use $35,000 of it to repay debts and $10,000 of it to re-invest in growth, you would be left with $5,000 to fund your Dream Lifestyle.

Five thousand dollars is better than zero, but it's not likely the amount you really need to live your Dream Lifestyle. If you're like most small business owners (who have not come into contact with the Found Money Roadmap Program), you wrongfully conclude that your Dream Lifestyle is unattainable.

But don't give up so fast.

Imagine that you could increase revenue by 10%. Don't worry about how, or even if it's possible for now. Just follow along with this thought process.

If your revenue went up by 10%, say by a price increase, your Gross Profit would go up as well. Because you haven't done anything to increase your direct costs all of that price increase would directly increase your gross profit.

Your financial results would now look like this:

Sales Revenue	$165,000 ($150,000 + ($150,000 x 10%))
Direct Costs	$ 55,000
Gross Profit	$110,000 (66.7%)
Overhead	$ 45,000
Net Profit	**$ 65,000**

(to fund repay debt, re-invest in growth, fund Dream Lifestyle)

In other words, by paying attention to your Gross Profit, you added an additional $15,000 toward funding your Dream Lifestyle.

Fifteen thousand dollars may not be enough to fund your entire Dream Lifestyle. The point is, however, that by making just one small change that affects your gross profit you have made a decent improvement in the ability of your business to fund your Dream Lifestyle.

When that one change is compounded with other changes, and compounded over time, the overall impact can be massive. In many cases, the impact can exceed your wildest expectations.

Calculating Gross Profit

Okay, so now you've seen why gross profit is important to you. Now let's get to the calculating Gross Profit for your business. After all, that's how you will be able to make your "financial results dance".

Before we get to the definition, let's get something straight about traditional accounting definitions of Gross Profit. Traditional accountants and textbooks have a slightly different version of Gross Profit than you will learn here.

Don't worry about it. Just be prepared that if you meet some "accounting purist" at a party (don't laugh, it could happen – maybe they took a wrong turn) to not get sucked into their philosophical debate.

That being said, let's talk briefly about the "normal" definition of Gross Profit. Traditionally gross profit is defined as being the amount left after subtracting the cost of sales from your sales revenue.

And there really isn't too much wrong with that traditional definition.

The problem with it is that it leaves the vast majority of small businesses out there feeling confused. That's because an awful lot of small businesses don't truly have "cost of sales" because they don't really purchase things to re-sell.

Many small businesses are service-type businesses and traditional Cost of Sales is largely irrelevant for them. But that doesn't mean that the concept and power of gross profit is irrelevant to them.

Because of that, the Found Money Roadmap Program uses "Direct Costs" instead of Cost of Sales when defining Gross Profit.

That being said, now, here is the formula for calculating Gross Profit:

Gross Profit = Sales Revenue – Direct Costs

That's Great, But What Are Direct Costs?

Direct costs, for our purposes (and I say that because we are going to look at direct costs in a way that is useful for us, not necessarily the "pure" accounting definition) are any expenses or costs that vary in proportion to your sales volume.

Direct costs can also be thought of as "marginal costs", although that isn't the "accounting purist" way of talking about them. The point is that direct costs can be thought of as those costs that will be incurred only when an additional sale is made.

Let's look at a health club as an example.

Suppose they have a salesperson on staff that is paid a monthly salary of $3,000 plus a commission of $250 on every new membership that is sold.

The monthly salary of $3,000 would NOT be considered a direct cost because it is incurred whether or not an additional membership is sold. However the commission of $250 would be treated as a direct cost since it only arises when a sale is made (it varies in proportion to sales volume).

Often service businesses have a relatively small amount of true direct costs. This means that they tend to have a fairly high gross profit on a percentage basis. So don't be overly concerned if you can't think of too many direct costs in your business.

Costs that are not considered to be direct costs in your business are deemed to be "overhead". This distinction will become important in the subsequent module.

Your Path To Great Financial Results

A solid understanding of Gross Profit is critical to the success of your efforts to increase your financial results. Gross Profit is a great tool for you to use to make business decisions and guide you in thoroughly understanding how your business makes money for you.

In subsequent chapters you will learn how to apply the power of Gross Profit to your business. And you will learn how to link it to your Dream Lifestyle and financial goals to help drive your decisions and create plans that will help you create the financial results you want from your business.

Chapter 8 – The Found Money Gross Profit Formula

In the previous chapter you were exposed to the basic concept of gross profit and learned how it is calculated (in its basic form).

Now it's time to dig deeper into the concept of Gross Profit and start building your skillset and ability to drive your financial results. What you will learn in this chapter is going to be used in the next one to identify your path to achieving your Dream Lifestyle that you identified earlier in this program.

Ready?

The Gross Profit Formula Re-Visited

You saw in the previous chapter how the basic Gross Profit formula works:

Gross Profit = Sales Revenue – Direct Costs

That formula for gross profit is useful just like that. But there is another way of defining gross profit – that is a much more helpful "formula" for helping you maximize and control your financial results.

Since this "advanced" way of looking at gross profit is part of the Found Money system, I have summoned every single ounce of my creative energy and called it….. the Found Money Gross Profit Formula.

Okay, so maybe not all that creative. I can admit it. But it's still a great name because it differentiates this way of looking at gross profit from the traditional way of defining it (the basic gross profit formula).

And defining gross profit in this new way allows you to make decisions and set targets that will actually CREATE the financial result you want from your business.

Get ready. Here's the Found Money Gross Profit formula:

Found Money Gross Profit = customers x frequency x gross profit per transaction

This formula tells us that the gross profit for your business depends directly on how many customers your business has, how often they buy from you, and how much gross profit each of those transactions generates.

And because gross profit is the "engine" that powers the financial results your business delivers to you, this formula is really the key to funding your Dream Lifestyle. In other words, the degree to which your business serves your Dream lifestyle depends directly on your ability to master the combination of these three elements of the Found Money Gross Profit Formula.

The Found Money Gross Profit Formula In Action

Let's look an example of two different businesses to clarify this concept. Some relevant data from each of the businesses is as follows:

	Business Alpha	Business Beta
(A) Number of Customers	1,000	370
(B) Frequency Per Year	0.5	6.0
(C) Average Gross Profit	$ 350	$79
Gross Profit (A x B x C)	$175,000	$175,380

This information tells us that we are looking at two businesses with completely different approaches and structures (two different business models). Business Alpha maintains a large number of customers who only buy something about every two years (frequency of 0.5 per year), but it's a bigger ticket item than Business Beta. Business Beta has far fewer customers (about one-third as many), but they buy a smaller ticket item much more frequently (about every two months).

But look at the end result. Both businesses return pretty much identical Gross Profit results. Each business has about $175,000 to cover overhead expenses, repay debts, re-invest in growth, and fund the owner's Dream lifestyles.

Harnessing the Found Money Gross Profit Formula

Another look at the Found Money Gross Profit Formula tells you there are really three (actually four) ways to create more gross profit (i.e. more money to repay debts, sustain operations, re-invest in growth, and fund your Dream Lifestyle) for your business:

- Get more customers;
- Sell to them more often;
- Increase the average gross profit of each transaction; or
- A combination of any of the above

Creating more money from your business is really a matter of leveraging your resources to the hilt. Every business has a limit on resources.

There's only so much time, energy, commitment, capital, and so that you and your team can muster. And the Found Money Gross Profit Formula is one of the best ways to figure out how best to leverage your resources to provide a specific financial outcome.

After all, your goal is to build a business that provides the Dream Lifestyle you desire and maximize your profit and cash flow. And I'm willing to bet your dream lifestyle doesn't include spending every spare moment of your time and every spare ounce of energy you've got trying to work harder and harder (like being on an increasingly fast treadmill).

I'm willing to bet that unless you are a true workaholic, your Dream Lifestyle involves just the opposite. It probably involves you having the time, money, free-time, and relaxed mental state to pursue whatever "non-business" interests you'd like. Fulfilling your dream lifestyle through your business demands that you focus on the part of the formula that gives you the most leverage.

Makes complete sense, doesn't it?

So given that, let's explore the 3 main ways to increase your gross profit and make more money in your business.

Get More Customers

Getting more customers is usually the first (and often the only) way many business owners (and even a lot of their advisors, such as accountants, marketers, and consultants) rely on to increase their profit and improve their Dream lifestyle.

They think they should crank up their advertising efforts. Or maybe offer some special sale and really "promote it hard". Paradoxically, this can often be a bad move.

Most media salespeople really encourage this method of increasing profits. The advertising reps for television stations, radio stations, newspapers, and Yellow Pages really try to tap into this angle as their default. They talk about how good their audience demographics match up with your business. They talk about how a great ad (usually created by their creative department) will get a bunch of people through your doors. They paint a wonderful picture of a booming business, filled with customers, if you'll just advertise with THEM.

And while there's not necessarily anything wrong with that approach, remember this. The media sales rep gets paid when they sell you advertising. They don't get paid to make you more profit.

But YOU get paid when your business makes money. Don't forget that. Ever!

This "Get More Customers" method of increasing profit has a few problems.

First of all, getting more customers means (sooner or later) you will need to increase your business infrastructure and overhead. As your business gets more customers to walk in, you will need to hire more team members, invest more in infrastructure (premises, computers, etc.) and possibly carry an increased investment in accounts receivable.

Over time, you might need to increase your overhead in other ways too. Perhaps you will need to rent larger space, buy more desks, add more service vehicles, or incur other additional expenses.

So this method of profit growth is an expensive one.

Another problem with the approach to growth is that it is completely "linear". That means that it is only possible to make as much additional profit as you and your team are able to work harder and more. That's a painful way to grow profit, and it's one that is completely at odds with you trying to maximize your leverage and have your business serve you and your Dream Lifestyle.

Sell To Existing Customers More Often (Increase Frequency)
Another way to increase your total net profit using the Found Money Formula is to increase how often your existing customers buy from you (frequency).

Sadly, this tactic is often completely ignored by business owners.

You already have a relationship with your existing customers. You already know who they are and how to contact them. Most importantly is that you already know what they have purchased from you in the past so you can draw some conclusions about what else they may need and want.

Selling to your existing customers is much less expensive compared to attracting and acquiring new ones. Getting new customers requires a big investment in time and money. It is one of the most expensive things you do in your business.

On the other hand, getting your existing customers to do business with you is significantly cheaper, faster, and much more certain than attracting new customers.

Yet despite all these advantages, many business owners have a complete blindness to growing their business in this manner.

For example, I was working with a business owner who had a large multi-location national company with several offices across the country.

When we did our analytical work, one of the patterns that emerged was that several national brand customers were doing business with the company – but only in one of its several locations.

The reason this was happening was that each individual branch manager was focused on their own branch's financial performance and was therefore targeting customers they could most easily acquire and service.

From the corporate perspective, however, this was leaving a tremendous amount of potential business "on the table". After all, if a national customer does business in one location, it makes sense they should also be approached to do business with the company's other locations.

The potential business this analysis uncovered was well over one million dollars annually.

The solution was to hire a key account salesperson who could work the list of national customers and leverage the relationship with one branch across all the branches.

This was a very effective and efficient way to get existing national customers to buy more from the company.

Beware, however, that even though it's easier and cheaper to increase frequency than to increase your number of customers, this tactic still suffers from the linearity problem.

Growing in this manner means your business will only be able to work as hard as you do (and are willing and able to). But because it's generally cheaper to increase frequency than to find new customers this tactic is preferable to the "get more customers" tactic.

Increase The Average Gross Profit Of A Transaction

Despite being almost always being ignored by business owners this method of increasing profit is the absolute BEST way to do it.

This method alone can virtually EXPLODE the money your business creates for you. It should be used as the cornerstone of creating financial results that serve your Dream Lifestyle.

This tactic involves either increasing your prices or selling additional items with each sale (cross-selling / up-selling), or both.

In every business there is more than a single product or service that can be sold. Many existing customers could really benefit by buying and using the additional products and services your business could provide.

For some reason, however, many businesses don't actively and systematically discuss their additional products and services with their customers. The lack of a systematic approach is a crime against your Dream lifestyle – it robs your business of its full potential.

Many business owners overlook the other things they could be offering each customer. This happens because these customers are overlooked because they are so familiar to the business.

The psychology is that because you are so familiar with the wide range of products and services your business COULD deliver you tend to take them for granted.

The tendency is to assume that, because you know about all your product and services, your customers know about them too, or have thought about them too. In other words, you assume your customers know what they want.

Often, however, customers don't know what they want.

So ask your customers what they are really trying to accomplish with their purchases. Then firmly suggest things you honestly believe they need and that they will benefit from. Tell them about ALL the things your business can provide for them.

Your customers will be impressed that you're thinking about them. Even if they don't want what you're suggesting, they will still know you, your team, and your business are proactively trying to make their lives better. And that will only deepen your relationship with your customers.

In many cases your customers will be delighted to find out about some of the other things you can offer them. As a result, they will become customers with a higher average gross profit.

Leveraging and Prioritizing the Found Money Gross Profit Formula

The Found Money Formula is a massively powerful tool to drive better business performance. It becomes a lever you can use to help your business serve you better and fund your Dream lifestyle.

The trick to get the most value out of the Found Money Gross Profit Formula is to know how each element can be used to create a specific Gross Profit target.

Let's start by compiling a basic hierarchy of tactics:
- The quickest way to raise your total gross profit is to increase prices which instantly increases gross profit per transaction;
- The next best method to increase gross profit is to systematically offer your customers other products and services during the existing sales process. This tactic also increases your gross profit per transaction;
- The next best method is to increase the frequency of your customer purchases;
- The least preferable way to increase total gross profit should be trying to attract new customers. This is where

most business owners start but it is actually the least effective and least favorable tactic.

Now let's take a deeper look into each of these approaches.

Increase Prices

Increasing prices provides massive leverage when it comes to increasing your gross profit and improving your financial results. It's just that simple!

When looking at increasing your prices it is critical that you focus on value to your customers. Value, from your customers' perspective is defined as follows:

$$\text{VALUE} = \frac{\underline{\text{Perceived Value of Benefits Received}}}{\text{Cost Required To Acquire Product}}$$

A quick look at this formula clearly shows that the fewer perceived benefits a customer gets from a transaction, the lower your price must be to make the sale.

To make a sale the "math" of the value equation every time you interact with a customer MUST be greater than 1.0. This is from the perspective of your customer. It doesn't matter one bit if YOU think the math works out to greater to 1.0

The problem occurs when you don't clearly define and describe the benefits for your customer or prospect. In that situation your customer is forced to assess the perceived benefits based on what they know and what they can easily figure out.

That usually leaves them with no choice other than to rely on price to gauge the value they are getting from your business.

By not clearly identifying the benefits, and making sure your customer knows what they are, YOU are forcing your customer to use price as their buying criteria. YOU are making them buy on price. YOU are training your customers to be your own problem.

Offer Other Products and Services At the Time Of Sale

This is the next easiest way to lift your total gross profit. You have already done all the really hard work.

You've taken the time and committed the money and effort to create a customer, provided a place of business for them to come to, team members to help them, and built a relationship with them. And you've accomplished all that by filling one of their needs with one of your products or services.

The odds are really, really high that the customer who is standing at the cash register at any particular time also has other needs that your business could fill. But the odds are just as high that particular customer isn't thinking about those other needs right now (and therefore isn't looking for a solution at the moment), or doesn't know your business can offer them.

Increase Frequency Of Purchases

This is the third best tactic in the hierarchy.

It is not as effective at increasing total gross profit as a price increase, and it's not as immediate as offering additional products and services to a customer buying something right now.

But it's a lot better than trying to find a new customer.

It's better because it leverages the existing relationships you've got with your customers. These people already know you, your team, your business, and your products and services it delivers (or at least some of your products and services).

You've already managed to break through all the marketing noise people are forced to endure every day. You've got an established relationship with these people.

That relationship means you can reach out and communicate with them easily and cheaply. In addition, your prior experience dealing with these people provides you the luxury of deciding if you really do want them to come back more often.

The ease with which your business can increase frequency of purchase – that fact that it is so simple and easy – often proves to be its downfall. Many business owners miss out on using the power of this technique because they are looking for something harder.

I don't know why this is, but an awful lot of business owners and managers seem to get so busy trying to knock the door down (the hard way to do it) that they don't even bother to try the doorknob (the easy way to do it). Now isn't that dumb?

Get More Customers

This is the last method of increasing total gross profit on our list. And it's the last method for a reason. It's the most expensive, most difficult and riskiest method, and takes the longest time period to produce any results.

And yet this is the method most business owners jump right into when they try to increase their profits. Frankly (and there's just no way to sugar-coat this) that's just plain DUMB! It doesn't make any sense AT ALL!

It doesn't make sense for three reasons:

1. It costs a lot of money, and despite your best efforts, it's almost impossible to make sure ONLY people in your most profitable and desirable customer target segment receive your message;

2. It's slow. Because usually it's necessary to reach potential customers many times to get your message to "stick" with them. And then you need to wait until they need (or think they need) what you sell; and

3. It's difficult. You can never be certain your efforts at attracting new customers are effectively received by your target. Or that they are interpreted in the way you want. Or that the recipient will fully understand what it is you want them to do.

I'm not saying this method should never be used. It can have a role in building a business that truly serves your Dream lifestyle. But this method must be carefully targeted at only attracting the right people after you have done a proper Customer Profitability Map (see the chapters later in this book).

You must also be prepared to wait the longest for any results if you use this method because it produces changes the slowest out of all the tactics above.

So while this tactic has a place in building your business, it should only be a small piece of the total picture. Don't fall into the trap of thinking that this method is the key to your success.

You can dramatically move your business toward serving your Dream lifestyle whether or not you use this method. So don't rely on just this one.

Chapter 9 – Your Found Money Breakeven

Now that you are thoroughly familiar with the concept of Gross Profit it's time to put that understanding to work. It's time to guide yourself toward creating a roadmap toward creating the financial results you want from your business to fund your Dream Lifestyle.

Applying your understanding of Gross Profit and the Found Money Gross Profit Formula give you the power to explore and test the impact of various changes in direct costs, gross profit, and sales volumes for your business. And that gives you the power to see the impact of those changes on the financial results your business creates for you.

And you can harness that power to also determine your exact path toward increasing your financial results to the point where your business serves your Dream Lifestyle.

Breakeven In Action

Let's jump right into an example so you can start developing an understanding of the power of the breakeven analysis.

Let's assume you have a business that has a Gross Profit of 40%. That means you have $40 dollars left out of each $100 in sales revenue, after factoring in your Direct Costs. Assume as well that the overhead for your business is $515,000 (overhead refers to all the expenses that are not Direct Costs – examples of overhead items are rent, utilities, advertising, management salaries, etc.).

Once we know just those few basic numbers, it is possible for you to quickly see what level of total sales volume your business will need to reach its "breakeven".

Breakeven is the point where the Gross Profit on total sales exactly offsets the overhead required to run the business. In other words, it's the point where sales volume reaches a level that provides your business with neither a net loss, nor a net profit.

The formula looks like this:

$$\text{Breakeven Sales Volume} = \frac{\text{Total Overhead}}{\text{Gross Margin (\%)}}$$

$$= \frac{\$515,000}{40\%}$$

$$= \underline{\$1,287,500}$$

So our breakeven analysis reveals that your business must generate $1,287,500 in total sales just to simply cover your overhead.

What Can We Do With That?

A lot of things. This number is critical to helping you map out how to create the financial results you want from your business.

Suppose that the overhead in the example above includes a recent large increase you made to your expenses anticipating increased growth. (this is common, for example, when a business increases its sales team and invests in base wages for additional sales people and sales managers.

Despite the best planning and most sincere beliefs that the anticipated growth will happen, if the business has never achieved total sales volume in excess of $1 million before then there's a significant level of risk. That risk becomes apparent when the Found Money Breakeven is applied to determine the sales level needed (in this case, a sales level well above anything achieved to date).

It's absolutely critical to do that because until your business reaches the $1.287 million in sales revenue it's going to lose money. Oh, and by the way, you need to achieve that level of sales revenue without discounting your prices.

If you discount your prices to drive sales your Gross Margin percentage will fall below the current level of 40%. This will require a higher level of sales than $1.287 million to break even.

Failure to realize this, and plan for it, could seriously jeopardize the profitability of your business. Or maybe even threaten its long-term future.

Three Steps To Your Found Money Roadmap

By following a three-step process you can give yourself the power to know where and how, you can dramatically increase the financial results your business creates.

You will be able to see an in-depth example, and follow along in a few moments. But as a preview, the three steps in the process that you will be using are:

1. Calculate your planned Found Money Overhead;
2. Find your Extreme Limits; and
3. Run Found Money Alternatives and select the most effective path for you and your business

A Mini-Case Study To Demonstrate

Suppose you have determined that your Dream lifestyle requires your business to generate an additional income of $100,000 a year for you and has you only working 3 days each week.

Suppose you also have decided that in order for you to only work 3 days a week, you're going to have to hire an excellent manager so your business continues to thrive while you're not there. You estimate that you will need to pay $85,000 a year for this person.

Finally, you also anticipate having to increase a few other areas of your existing operation that are going to require you to add another $25,000 to your current overhead of $125,000 per year.

And just a few more data items for our example – assume your business has current gross margin of 40%, has 1,000 customers with a frequency of 0.5 (they buy once every two years, on average), and an average gross margin per transaction of $350.

That's a lot of detail, I know. But that's exactly the information you are going to have to pull out of your business, and the information gathering process you absolutely MUST go through, if you plan to create a business that serves you.

Now let's apply what you have learned and run through the steps of creating your Found Money Marketing Roadmap.

Step 1 - Calculate your Planned Found Money Overhead

Add your planned overhead increases (your additional income requirement, the new manager, and other anticipated increases) needed to create a business that serves your Dream lifestyle to your existing overhead.

This revised total overhead number is called your Found Money Overhead.

In this case that total is as follows:

Extra owner compensation	$100,000
Manager required	$ 85,000
Additional overhead	$ 25,000
Existing overhead	$125,000
Total Found Money Overhead	**$335,000**

Step 2 - Find The Extreme Limits

The next step is to apply the Found Money Formula to test the 3 extreme limits that would still result in a Found Money Breakeven. This can be done by trial and error or (this is a better option) by using the Found Money online app you can find at our website, www.BizDogGroup.com

The way to find the 3 extremes is to hold two of the three factors in the Found Money Formula the same as their current values and change only the remaining factor until you achieve the Found Money Breakeven.

In our example the 3 extreme limits are what you see on below:

	Current Base	Customer Focus	Frequency Focus	Average Profit Focus
Customers	1,000	1,916	1,000	1,000
Frequency	0.5	0.5	0.96	0.5
Avg. Gross Profit	$350	$350	$350	$670

Step 3 - Identify Alternatives And Select The Best One For Your Business

Of course relying on only one of these three options will no doubt be very difficult. Relying on new customers alone (even though that's the approach most business owners seem to accept by default) would require the number of customers to almost double.

Can you even imagine what that would do the required level of staffing, workload and infrastructure?

Relying only on increasing the customer frequency would prove just as problematic. Doubling the frequency is essentially the same (logistically speaking) as doubling the number of customers. It's probably just not possible. And it is possible it's going to cause the same problems and doubling the number of customers.

Increasing average profit by 91% would require a massive price increase or massive decrease in costs. And while I'm a huge fan of price increases, it's just not possible to get increases that are that large and still have any business left.

But the situation is anything but hopeless if you consider a blending of the elements over time. If it is carefully planned out and considered.

For example, assume you decide you want to achieve your Dream lifestyle over a three-year period. After all, it's your Dream lifestyle. And that means it's probably a stretch from where you find yourself and your business right now. And if it's not a big stretch then you haven't created a big enough dream yet.

A dream that is an appropriately large stretch is one that you are not going to be able to achieve instantly. But it is possible to make large gains toward that outcome in a short period of time by using the concepts in this book.

So let's take a more balanced approach and look at one possible way your Found Money Formula could be transformed over the 3 year period for your Dream lifestyle plan.

What if you decided to target an increase of 7.5% in each of the three elements of your Found Money Formula for the next three years. What would happen to your total gross profit?

Take a look below:

	Current	Year 1	Year 2	Year 3
Customers	1,000	1,075	1,156	1,243
Frequency	0.5	0.54	0.58	0.62
Average Gross Margin	$350	$376.25	$404.47	$434.80
Total Gross Profit	$175,000	$217,402	$277,078	$335,517

And presto!! There you have it!!

A simple, consistent increase of 7.5% each year in each element of your Found Money Formula creates an increase of 92% over the base case total gross profit, over a three-year period.

And even more important is that that steady increase results in a gross profit that covers your Found Money Overhead. And remember, your Found Money Overhead was built around providing you an additional $100,000 in personal income, and hiring a manager so you only had to work 3 days per week.

You're there! How totally cool is that?

Over a short three-year period, taking consistent actions (and tracking your results) to provide a 7.5% increase in each of the three elements of your Found Money Formula will create a whopping 92% increase in gross profit. And since that 92% increase provides your business with a Found Money Breakeven, that means your business will actually be able to provide you with your Dream lifestyle (that you determined) in a three-year period.

Chapter 10 – Your Customer Profitability Map

I like to think of every business as being a lot like the castles you see in old movies. In those movies, the castles were created by the king (actually he envisioned it, and then used skilled people to actually do the heavy work, but no matter). And the king decided who would be allowed to come inside the castle walls.

If someone wasn't the kind of person the ruler wished to have around, that person simply wouldn't be allowed in.

And at the same time, there were always hostile forces who wanted to get inside the castle, take it over, and change the peaceful existence the ruler maintained.

To defend against unwanted people coming in (either hostile or simply undesirable), the castles had walls to keep them out, and a drawbridge to strictly control who could get inside. And the only ones who got inside were people the ruler liked, and wanted to be inside.

The drawbridge was the access point that was used to control who was allowed inside and who was prevented from getting in.

Your Very Own Drawbridge

In your business, you also have a drawbridge that can be used to determine who gets inside. You can control who gets the privilege of working with you and your team, if you have the courage to exercise that control.

And if you have any hopes of building a business that maximizes your profit, fun, and free-time, and serves your Dream lifestyle, you simply MUST exercise that control. Get used to it because your ultimate success, happiness, and lifestyle depend on it.

For example, near my house there is a fantastic little place called The Blues Can. It has live blues bands that are amazing every night it's open. The place looks like it hasn't been changed in 50 years from the outside, and from the inside.

However, that's completely fine. Because this isn't the kind of place you go "to be seen" – you know the kind. At The Blues Can, you can wear a suit and tie, but you're more likely going to fit in if you show up in jeans and a comfortable shirt.

The Blues Can focuses on attracting customers who want fantastic live music, reasonable prices on drinks, and an utter lack of pretension. If you're looking for that you've found your nirvana.

And if you're not, that's completely fine as well because The Blues Can is quite comfortable with you going somewhere else to be ultra hip.

Everything The Blues Can does is designed to get a specific customer type through their doors, and to keep customers who aren't a good fit going somewhere else.

Your Customer Profitability Map

But how do you decide who YOU should let into YOUR business?

After all, like the old castles, there are all sorts of different people you *could* allow inside. And if you don't consciously decide who gets in, you're going to find your business overrun with barbarians and other unsavory types (okay, maybe not quite that bad, but you won't have control over your business and its financial results).

The Customer Profitability Map is a powerful tool to help you decide who you should allow inside.

The Customer Profitability Map (CPM), at its core, is a way of sorting and ranking the customers for any business. And when done in the way the CPM does it, you and your team can quickly uncover vital information that will help you drive your business toward serving your Dream lifestyle.

The CPM uses two criteria. The first is the profitability of each customer. This one is a numeric fact that you obtain from your business records. The second one is a subjective one that is called the Resonance Score.

We will discuss these two criteria in more detail in a little bit, but first let me give you a "big picture" example to convince you to pay attention to this stuff.

An Example Of The Customer Profitability Map

Assume you own a company that has hired me to help understand where it should focus its efforts to maximize profit, fun, and free-time. As part of the process, you have ranked all the customers according to their profitability, and their Resonance Score (you are going to find out a lot more about Resonance Scores, what they are, and how to do them very shortly – so don't worry about the new term at this moment).

On the next page is what your customer base looks like when it's plotted this way.

Customer Profitability Plot

Profitability vs *Resonance Score* (scatter plot, Profitability axis 0–80, Resonance Score axis 1–10)

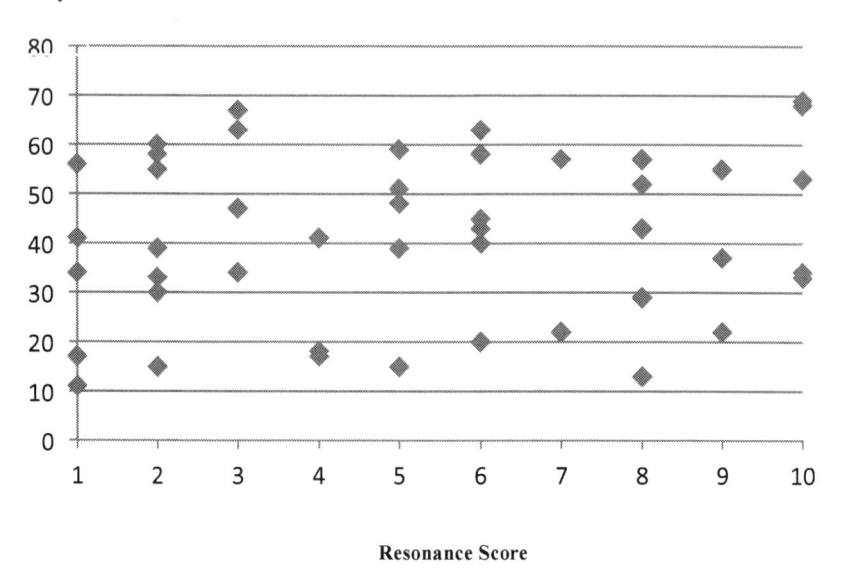

So what you say?

It's just an ugly plot of a bunch of dots, right?

Absolutely correct. It's useless!

But the good news is that this *isn't* the Customer Profitability Map (CPM) – it's only the first step in creating it.

Now we assign some categories to this chart to give it meaning. THEN we will have converted the data set into a very useful Customer Profitability Map.

Before we do that, let's stop and consider what the data actually is telling us.

The scale on the left shows the profitability of each customer. The higher up toward the top of the chart a customer is, the more profitable they are for you compared to the rest of your customers.

The scale across the bottom of the chart shows each customer's Resonance Ranking. This is a score of between 1 and 10 you give each of your customers that captures how well they "fit in" with your business, your team, and your approach to business. It attempts to rank how pleasant they are to work with.

Resonance Score

Resonance Score is such a fundamental element of the CPM that it deserves some extra attention to make sure you fully understand it, and how to create it.

The Resonance Score for any customer is a subjective number between 1 and 10 that you give each customer based on things such as:
- How pleasant they are to deal with
- How much they respect you and your team
- How respectful of your time (and that of your team)
- Are their expectations, and demands of your business, reasonable?
- Are they "fun" to deal with?
- Do they allow you, your team, and your business to utilize your full talents?
- Do they treat you as "equals" or as "servants"?

The Resonance Score is a subjective measure of the "gut feel" you and your team have about how well a particular customer "clicks" with your business.

Customers who achieve a higher score are ones that are much more pleasant to deal with, who value you, your team, and what your business does for them, etc.

Back To The Customer Profitability Plot

So let's return to the plot of the customer data we looked at previously. If we take this data, and break it into 4 distinct quadrants, we will get the chart that follows:

Customer Profitability Map

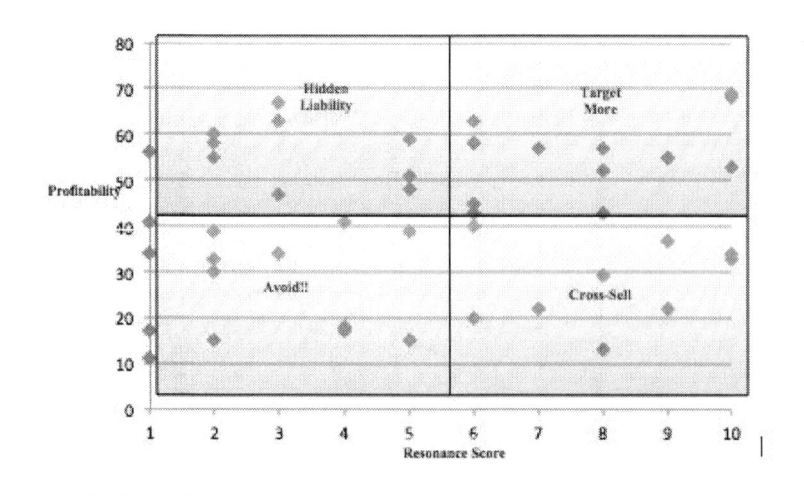

This is your Customer Profitability Map (CPM)!

I've named each quadrant to help describe the impact customers in that part of the chart have on your business and its relevance to creating your Dream lifestyle. Each name is designed to both describe the customers who fall into each quadrant, and to serve as a reminder for you whenever you think about your business and your customers.

Now let's talk about the customers in each of the quadrants.

Hidden Liability
These are customers that are quite profitable for your business but have low resonance scores. In other words the profit they generate comes at a fairly high price. And that "price" is reflected in their low Resonance Scores.

Perhaps these customers are too demanding, put unrealistic and unfair demands on you and your team, or are chronically grumbling about prices, service, your team, etc. Whatever the reason, the fact that they have a low Resonance Score suggests they really don't "click" with you, your business, and your team.

These are the type of customers who "always feel like work". You know the feeling. It just always seems that they aren't truly valuing your business, its products, services, and team. And it always feels "unnatural" or unpleasant to deal with them. There's just no connection.

Their category is given the name, "Hidden Liability" because they represent a hidden danger for your business. Their low Resonance Scores make it likely they will switch to another competitive business as soon as they see the opportunity, or find something that they perceive to be better.

The fact that they will ultimately leave your business, itself, isn't a bad thing. Remember, their low Resonance Scores generally make them emotionally draining and difficult to serve.

But the fact that they are also highly profitable is what gives rise to the Hidden Liability. Because when they do finally switch to a competitor, the business loses quite a significant amount of profit along with them. And that "profit hole" is what gives rise to the Hidden Liability.

They are a chunk of profit just waiting to evaporate from your business. And that's not a good thing, is it?

Avoid!!
Customers in this quadrant are those who don't really have anything going for them. Okay, that's probably a bit harsh. But it's true, from the point of view of the Customer Profitability Map. After all, they are among the least profitable customers, AND they have low Resonance Scores.

In other words, they are a "pain" to deal with (low Resonance Scores), and even worse than that, they aren't even worth the effort because they are among your least profitable customers.

These people are absolute poison to your business.

They can bog your business down under a punishing load of low profit work, and strangle your business and your team to the point where you can't even take care of the clients who really do make you money and have high Resonance Scores. These customers can literally hijack your business, and hold your profit, fun, and free time hostage.

Your success, happiness, and Dream lifestyle absolutely demand that you do everything in your power to make sure you don't deal with these people. Don't let them in your front door. Don't waste a minute of time, or an ounce of effort trying to attract, or even talk to these people.

And if you've got any of them as customers right now (and every business, sadly, has many) GET RID OF THEM. These are the people who must never be allowed to get past your drawbridge. And if you find any of these people inside your business, toss them out.

And toss them out immediately!

<u>Cross-Sell</u>
This quadrant represents a ton of potential for your business and your Dream lifestyle. In fact, I've worked with business owners who discovered that they were able to create financial results that funded their Dream Lifestyle just from taking advantage of the opportunities in this quadrant.

Customers in this quadrant are delightful to work with.

They have high Resonance Scores. And that means they enjoy your business, respect you and your team, and are generally quite pleasant to work with.

They sound like a dream, and when it comes to "clicking" with you, your business, and your team they really are a dream. But they aren't' perfect, by any stretch. At least for now.

The "dirty little secret" these customers hide (but not anymore, because you've found them out) is that they aren't very profitable.

But guess what?

They don't have to stay unprofitable. And they won't stat unprofitable any more.

The fact that these customers have a high Resonance Score means they can usually be converted into much more profitable customers for any business.

The established relationship and connection they have with you, your team, and your business is a positive and strong (that's why they have high Resonance Scores). And that provides a huge opportunity to cross-sell them additional products and services that the business might be able to provide them. In many cases, it becomes apparent that these customers had no idea about all the additional products and services the business could offer.

Target More
These are the "jewel-box" clients for your business. They have a great relationship with your business, they value your products and services, and they value your team.

AND, they are among your most profitable customers.

Hmmmmm.

Let's see, fun to deal with, and profitable.

These are people we want more of!

Guard Your Drawbridge

Okay, now we've categorized the customers for this business, and created its CPM. Because of that, it suddenly gets real easy to effectively plan and execute various tactics to move toward a business that serves your Dream lifestyle.

Because the characteristics of customers in each category are different, the strategies and tactics used for each category should be (in fact MUST be) different. The goals for each category are different. And that means they need to be dealt with using different techniques and approaches.

Remember, not everyone deserves to get past your drawbridge. And not everyone who has gotten past it deserves to stay inside.

Chapter 11 – Analyzing Your Customer Profitability Map

Now that you've created you Customer Profitability Map it's time to start using it. You are going to dig deep and uncover potential problems and hidden opportunities.

In a short period of time, you're going to discover:
- how many customers your business is at risk of losing to a competitor
- how much of your profits would likely evaporate if your business faced any new competitive pressures
- how much of your profits are at risk if one of your existing competitors makes a sudden move in your marketplace
- how much extra profit a potential marketing tactic might generate (or should generate)
- what kind of realistic and measurable results you should demand from your marketing tactics
- Which of your existing marketing tactics should be continued, and which should be immediately stopped.

It might sound a little bit like science fiction, but a careful analysis of your Customer Profitability Map will tell you all those things. And more.

Of course, there is a caveat. You will need to have created an accurate Customer Profitability Map.

If you "fluffed" a bunch of data and didn't take the time to truly drill down into your business to get solid data (and I know that's a chore in some cases), your Customer Profitability Map is not going to be anything more than a cute exercise.

There are 4 main analyses to be done on your Customer Profitability Map. They are listed below, and will be discussed more fully in a few moments. For the moment, we're just going to list them and give you a quick description of what each is, and what it does.

Total Quadrant Weighting.

This shows the proportion of customers your business has in each of the four quadrants. It provides a powerful look at the risks and opportunities that currently exist in your business. This is the starting point to clearly find out where your business is right now.

Profit At Risk.

This measure shows the amount of profit your business could quickly lose if faced with competitive attacks in your market. It's an estimate because it uses the quadrant average, and there is no way of knowing exactly how much such a loss would be, until it occurs. But it's still tremendously useful to know the size of this at-risk profit.

Cross-Sell Potential.

This measure shows how much "early yardage" your business has just waiting to be tapped. It shows what kind of "lost profits" you could quickly and easily capitalize on to generate profit and cash flow to sustain the rest of your change efforts.

This measure relies on the fact that it's practically a guarantee that many of your customers could, and would, buy more things from you, if you only offered them to them.

Profit replacement potential.

This measure tells you how much new profit your business could quickly create by getting rid of customers in the Avoid quadrant.

Why does analyzing your Customer Profitability Map matter to you?

If you don't do it you will never realize the full potential of your business (maximize the profit, fun and free-time you get). Unless you just get plain lucky (which is very unlikely) it is practically impossible for your business to serve your Dream lifestyle without harnessing the power of the CPM.

Customer Profitability Map Walk-Through

Let's look at a sample company and follow how the Customer Profitability Map works. The owners of this business, along with their team, have done the work and come up with the profitability and a consensus Resonance Score for each of their customers.

Total Quadrant Weighting
This is simply the proportion of your total customers who fall into each of the four quadrants. In this case, the Total Quadrant Weighting looks like what you see on the following page:

CPM Total Quadrant Weighting

Hidden Liability	**Target More**
17%	22%
Avoid!!	**Cross-Sell**
35%	26%

Note that even though you have only taken the first step in the CPM Analysis, you've already got some very powerful, interesting and useful information about the business. From just this one part of the analysis we know the following:

1. Just over half (52% - the total of the Hidden Liability and Avoid! quadrants) of all the customers for this business have low Resonance Scores.

   Experience has shown that customers who have low Resonance Scores tend to take a lot more than their proportionate share time and resources. In other words, the 52% of all customers who have low Resonance Scores and very likely consume much more than 52% of the capacity this business has.

   A lot of time and effort is being sucked up by customers who don't "click" well with the business.

2. Over one-third of all the customers fall into the Avoid! quadrant. They have low Resonance Scores, which means they are difficult to deal with, and don't really respect the business owner and the team. And to add insult to injury, these people are also among the least profitable of all the customers this business has.

It's no exaggeration, at all, to say that this business would be better off if it got rid of all these people. Valuable resources would be almost instantly freed up, and time and attention could be focused on cross-selling and attracting new customers who would be a better fit.

Following the same logic of the first point, the customers in this quadrant suck up way more than one-third of the available resources. And they give nothing but pain and low profit in return.

In case I'm not being clear enough, let me say it another way…GET RID OF THESE PEOPLE!!!!!

3. Less than a quarter of all customers fall into the Target More quadrant.

   This is actually quite shocking when you think about it. It means fewer than one out of four customers are BOTH great to deal with (high Resonance Score) and highly profitable for the business.

   Said another way, this means that over 75% of customers are NOT the best ones for this business. Talk about a tragedy!

4. Slightly more than one quarter of all the customers are great to deal with (high Resonance Score), but are in the bottom half of profitability, which puts them in the Cross-Sell quadrant

   This means that roughly one out of four customers are like uncut diamonds. They are potentially valuable if the right actions are taken to polish them and transform them into true gems.

   This represents an absolutely HUGE opportunity to build quick cash flow and profits to sustain change efforts!

Profit At Risk

Now let's take a look at how much profit could potentially evaporate if this business were to face a new, aggressive competitor, or even a vigorous competitive attack from an existing competitor.

Looking at the Hidden Liability quadrant, we see 17% of all customers fall into this quadrant. That number, by itself, doesn't tell us anything about the Profit At Risk number. But it will in a moment.

You don't see it here, but the actual customer data showed the total gross profit from customers in this quadrant for the last year totaled $46,900 (this isn't given in the data set but you could get it from the accounting records for the business). Of course, when you do your own analysis, you will have this information ready to go.

And since each customer in this quadrant has a low Resonance Score, their relationship with the business is tenuous. These customers are the most likely to switch to another company if they are given the opportunity, and encouragement. Most often this motivation comes from a new competitor, or an existing competitor who makes a strategic change.

In the case of customers in the Avoid! quadrant, such an exodus wouldn't really hurt the business that much. After all, these customers don't yield much of a profit. But there is a huge potential loss if customers in the Hidden Liability quadrant leave.

The fact that they are highly profitable for the business means that losing them, while perhaps emotionally satisfying (due to their low Resonance Scores), would be damaging in the short-term.

Cross-Sell Potential
This part of the analysis looks at how much profit the business stands to gain by moving customers in the Cross-Sell quadrant to

the mid-point profitability of the customers in your Target More quadrant.

After all, your Cross-Sell quadrant customers are people who have high Resonance Scores. You enjoy them, get along well with them, and they most likely value and respect your business and your team.

They are worth keeping.

And because of that, it's definitely worth trying to increase the level of profitability they deliver to the business.

This analysis involves a few simple steps:

1. Determine the average profit for customers in this quadrant. In the example data the total gross profit for customers in this quadrant was $38,100 with a total of 12 customers in this quadrant. The average gross profit per customer in this quadrant is, therefore, $3,175.

2. Determine the average profit for customers in the Target More quadrant. In the example, the total gross profit for all Target More customers is $58,700 with a total of 10 customers in the quadrant. This gives an average gross profit per customer is $5,870.

3. Calculate the difference between the two average values. The difference in this case is $2,695 ($5,870 - $3,175). We will call this number the Cross-Sell Spread.

4. Multiply the Cross-Sell Spread by the total number of customers in the Cross-Sell quadrant. In this case, multiplying the 12 customers in the quadrant by the Cross-Sell Spread of $2,695 gives us a value of $32,340.

And there you have the Cross-Sell Potential for this business.

We now know that if the business could the profitability of each customer in the Cross-Sell quadrant to the average profitability for customers in the Target More quadrant, the business would increase its total gross profit by $32,340!!

Of course it's not realistic to assume that every single Cross-Sell customer could be moved to that level (although I'd sincerely argue that they should be). But even if the business could achieve 50% of that potential, there's still over $16,000 additional gross profit that could be realized. And that would represent an amazing 42% increase over the current profitability of those same customers!!!.

Profit Replacement Potential
This calculation is similar to the Cross-Sell Potential we just covered.

The idea behind this measure is that any customers in Quadrant 3 (Avoid! quadrant members) really need to be fired. They contribute little net profit to your business, and they have low Resonance Scores.

So to summarize it another way customers in the Avoid! quadrant just aren't worth the effort required to have them around. Pure and simple – they're not worth it.

Just consider all the time these customers take away from you and your team. It's so common for customers in the Avoid! quadrant to be the largest consumers of the one resource you can never get more of – time.

These people tend to be the ones who are always nagging about small things. And often, these same customers are the ones who demand immediate action, even when their timeline just isn't feasible.

In addition to consuming large amounts of time, these customers suck an awful lot of emotional energy out of you and your team. Because they have low Resonance Scores, they are difficult to deal with. The relationship they have with the business is strained, and feels like work.

Because it is.

They just don't "click" with you, your team, and your business.

So imagine if a business could get rid of ALL the customers in the Avoid! quadrant. Think about how much time would be freed-up. How much emotional energy would be freed-up by not having to waste any of it dealing with these people?

What would you do with all the freed-up time, and emotional energy?

If you're like most business owners, you'd make sure you spent a good chunk of the newly found time with your best customers (your Target Mores). And you could use some of that time to carefully target and pursue new customers who would fit into your Target More quadrant.

So here's how to do the calculation of the Profit Replacement measure:
1. Determine the average net profit for customers in the Avoid! quadrant. In this example, the total gross profit of customers in this quadrant was $47,900 with a total of 16

customers in the quadrant. The average gross profit for the Avoid! quadrant is $2,994.

2. Determine the average net profit provided for customers in the Target More quadrant. In our example, the total profit for the quadrant was $58,700 with 10 customers, for an average profit of $5,870.

3. Calculate the "quadrant-spread" between these two numbers. In this case, the spread is $2,876 ($5,870 - $2,994).

4. Estimate how much time, on average, gets spent on a typical customer from the Avoid! quadrant. This is a subjective guess in many cases, but do your best. In our example, the owner estimated that a typical customer in the Avoid! consumed 35 hours over the course of a year.

5. Estimate how much time, on average, gets spent on a typical customer from the Target More quadrant. In the example, the business owner figured it was about 12 hours a year.

6. Divide the time estimate for the typical Avoid! customer by the time estimate for a typical Target More customers. In this case, the resulting value is 2.9 (35 hours / 12 hours).

This is the theoretical number of new Target More customers that could be served for every single customer from the Avoid! quadrant the business could get rid of.

But it's very unlikely that the entire time freed up by firing Avoid! customers would be spent on new Target More customers. Most likely a portion of the "found" time and resources would be spent on other projects, and improving relationships with existing customers in other quadrants.

Because of that fact, pick some percentage of the freed up time that could realistically be spent attracting and working with new Target More customers. In the example, the business owner used 50% (they felt half of the freed up time would be spent on new Target More customers).

7. Now multiply the "quadrant-spread" from Step 3 by the time "multiplier" from Step 6, and multiply that by the percentage estimated in Step 7. And then multiply the value obtained by the number of total customers in the Avoid! quadrant.

In the example, the step would give a result of $66,723 ($2,876 x 2.9 x 50% x 16 = $66,723!!!)

What does this number mean?

In our example, the Profit Replacement Potential measure shows that if the business owner fired all 16 of the customers in the Avoid! quadrant, and devoted 50% of the freed-up time to acquiring new customers in the Target More quadrant, total gross profit would shoot up by a whopping $66,723.

Another way of looking at is to think about what each of those Avoid! customers is costing the business. And yes, they are costing the business. Because until they are fired, they will continue to suck up time and emotional energy, and return little net profit.

So if the Profit Replacement Potential analysis shows the business would be better off by almost $67,000 if it fired its Avoid! customers, and if the current Avoid! customers are creating a scarcity of resources and capacity, then each customer in the Avoid! quadrant is currently COSTING the business $4,187 in lost profit potential!!!!!

Chapter 12 – CSF's, KPI's, and QuickFailing for Success

Controlling and improving the financial results your business creates can be really simple - if you let it be. Sadly, however, most business owners seem almost to go out of their way to make it way more difficult than it needs to be.

Successfully creating a specific financial result is a matter of "failing forward".

What does that mean?

It means that producing a specific financial result is nothing more than planning what needs to happen to produce that result (i.e. which customers, what products and services, what prices, etc). Then you identify the gap between those areas right now in your business, and where they need to be to create the desired financial result.

Once you have identified the gaps you can start changing your activities and tactics in an effort to move toward your desired results.

That may sound ridiculously simple and naive.

It really isn't – but I'll admit that it does sound that way.

The reason it sounds so naïve is that when most business owners and leaders attempt to make changes to improve their financial results, they do it from "pure guesswork" and without any way of quickly knowing if it is working.

That approach forces them to wait until their "experiments" are translated into financial results and those financial results are able to be recorded. The problem is that by that point in time, it is too late to make any changes.

For example, suppose you do the "traditional thing" and sign up for a twelve month radio ad package. The radio station will work with you to create your ads, and then they will run them in rotation, and charge you (a lot, usually) for the service.

At the end of the quarter, or year (most likely) you take a look at sales, net income, and advertising expenses on your financial statements. Then you "decide" if it was "worth it" or not.

That approach is really useless for you. If it didn't work, you've already spent money for the whole year and, unless you've got a time machine in your closet, there is no way to change it.

Imagine if, instead of that approach, you could confidently try new tactics quarterly, monthly, weekly, even daily. And that you would know the risk up front, and would also know just as quickly if the results were moving you toward your desired financial result.

You Can Do Just That Very Thing

Now that you have gone through the rest of the concepts in this book you can apply the power of Critical Success Factors, Key Performance Indicators, and Quick Failing to turbo-charge your efforts (and results).

With these things it becomes a relatively easy process to drive your business toward producing those very results.

Critical Success Factors

What are Critical Success Factors (CSF's)?

CSF's are the relatively few things that you ABSOLUTELY must get right in your business if you are to combine the people and activities in your business to produce the financial result you want.

These are things that must happen, under each and every circumstance.

If they don't happen, your desired financial results won't happen. It's that simple.

For example, suppose you own a wedding photography studio. What might some of the CSF's be for the business? It's hard to know without a more detailed knowledge of the business but here are some CSF's that most likely apply:
- Good quality photos
- On time to event
- No equipment failures
- No "shortages" of critical supplies
- No booking problems
- Getting bookings
- Getting paid

There's probably a few more, but not many. Think about it for a moment. When this wedding photography business is stripped to its basic elements, there's only about 7 things it MUST get absolutely right in order to delight its target customers, sell its services, and produce the financial result the owner wants.

Now, each one of those CSF's has several different elements. But identifying the CSF's creates a simplified structure for your business. Clearly identified CSF's allow you to start creating "systems" to ensure those CSF's are consistently met.

And as long as you continue to ensure that the small number of CSF's continues to happen you can be confident your business will continue to move toward serving your Dream Lifestyle.

Mapping Your Business To Find CSF's

A very useful tool to help you identify your CSF's is the Customer Cycle Map. And while the name might conjure images of complex industrial engineering drawings it's not like that at all.

It's actually quite simple.

A Customer Cycle Map is simply a way for you to think about each step in your regular business cycle. Start at the point where a customer first becomes aware of your business and follow all the steps through to the point where the customer is delighted by their experience and the product or service they receive.

Mapping it out this way provides a way of visually thinking through each part of your business. Back to the wedding photographer example. If they were to draw their Customer Cycle Map, it might look something like this:

Wedding Photography Customer Cycle Map

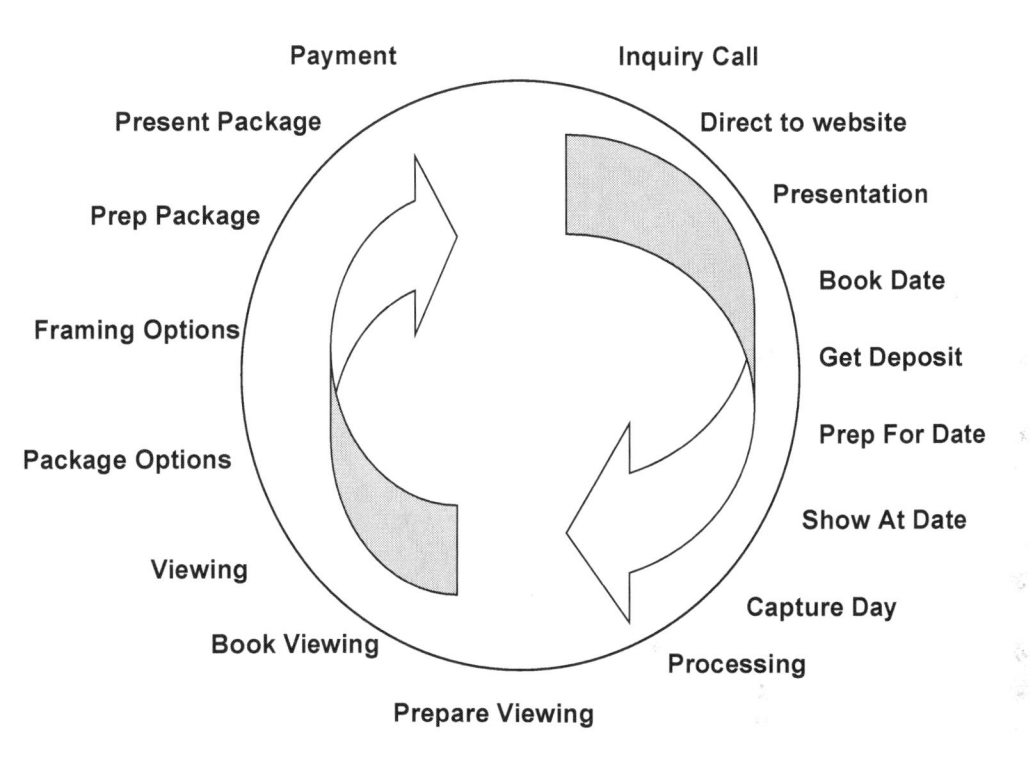

Cycle diagram with the following stages (clockwise from top):

- Payment
- Present Package
- Prep Package
- Framing Options
- Package Options
- Viewing
- Book Viewing
- Prepare Viewing
- Processing
- Capture Day
- Show At Date
- Prep For Date
- Get Deposit
- Book Date
- Presentation
- Direct to website
- Inquiry Call

Looking at this cycle map, some CSF's become apparent rather quickly.

Converting inquiries into booked engagements / contracts is the first obvious one. After all, if the photographer doesn't get any actual bookings, the business won't succeed.

Another CSF that comes out the cycle map (there are several, but we'll just take a look at two of them) is selling packages from the viewing. This is where all the effort, creativity, and expertise of the photographer is transformed into revenue, profit, and cash flow. If this step is botched, financial results will suffer (as well as the owner's Dream Lifestyle).

Key Performance Indicators

Key Performance Indicators (KPI's) are measures that indicate how well the CSF's for your business are being met. They provide leading indicators of how well your business is on track to achieve your Dream Lifestyle.

The best KPI's are almost always non-financial. The reason is that it simply takes too long for the impact to show up in the financial results. KPI's are measures of things *that will CREATE a financial result*, but tell you in advance if the financial result will be on target or not.

By developing and using KPI's you can essentially measure what the financial results will be, in "real time". That gives you the power to make changes if certain tactics or activities are indicating that the desired financial targets will be missed if the status quo continues.

In the wedding photographer example, it's clear that an increase in bookings will create increased revenue (and increased net profit). But the financial outcome (increased net profit) is a lagging indicator because it happens "after the fact". By that I mean if revenue does not increase in a certain period, the owner and team won't know that until AFTER the period is over. By then, however, it's history and can't be "retroactively" changed.

However, using the "people and activities" viewpoint, we can identify some KPI's that will measure progress toward achieving the owner's Dream Lifestyle. And we will be able to monitor and assess the financial results while they are being created!

Assume, for example, that the wedding photographer has historically booked 24 weddings each year. And assume that the business has historically received 20 phone enquiries each week from people looking to hire a wedding photographer.

We've identified "getting clients" as one of the CSF's for the business. So what might be a KPI that indicates how well that CSF is being met? One possible KPI would be the call conversion rate. This KPI compares the number of appointments booked to the number of enquiry calls received.

Continuing with our example, if the photographer booked 5 presentations a week from the 20 enquiry calls the call conversion rate would be 25%. In other words, for every 4 phone enquiries received, on average 1 presentation would be booked.

Call conversion rate is a KPI. It is a measure of how well the relevant CSF (getting customers) is being accomplished. It predicts what the financial outcome will be and is therefore a leading indicator.

Let's continue to follow this through to make it clear.

We know 20 enquiry calls per week are historically received. Assuming a couple of weeks per year for vacation, holidays, etc. that translates into 1,000 enquiry calls per year. If the historical call conversion rate was 25%, that means the photographer would have about 250 presentations over the course of a year. And we have already established that the photographer books 24 weddings in an average year (approximately a 10% booking to presentation rate).

This process can be presented visually by thinking of a funnel like this:

Call Conversion Funnel

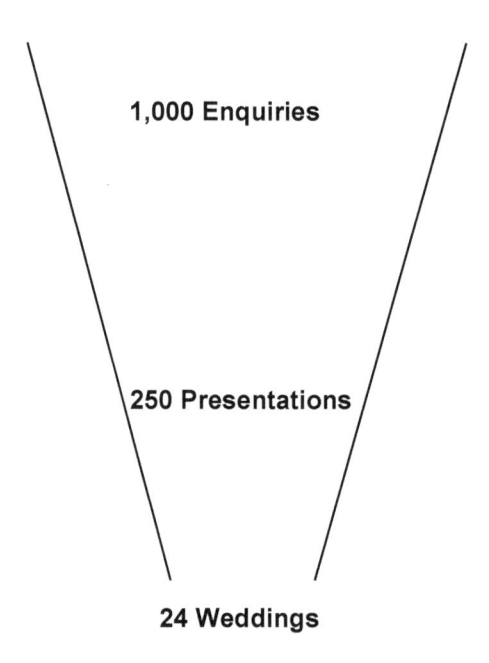

1,000 Enquiries

250 Presentations

24 Weddings

So, in other words, we know if the enquiry call conversion rate is 25% and the number of enquiries is 20 per week, that the business is on target to duplicate its historical sales revenue.

How can that help the photographer improve the business and move it toward serving his Dream Lifestyle? Let's take a look. Suppose each wedding nets the photographer $4,000 in profit. In an average year (where he had 24 weddings), he would realize a net profit of $96,000.

Now what if the photographer's Dream Lifestyle required him to make a profit of $124,000. If he maintained his $4,000 profit per wedding it would require him to have 31 weddings in the year (up from the 24 he historically did).

So what does the photographer need to do? Should he run out and start advertising? That might work, but it might not. It's also likely to be very expensive.

By focusing on using KPI's it's entirely possible that the photographer can achieve this $28,000 increase in profit. At NO, or VERY LITTLE additional cost.

Let's revisit the KPI's for this business. What are the 2 ways the photographer can get 31 weddings booked, without much additional effort?

All that needs to happen is one of the following:
Convert 31% of Enquiry Calls into Presentations. This assumes that the 10% conversion from Presentations to Bookings continues to apply, or
Convert 12.4% of Presentations into bookings. This assumes that the 25% Enquiry to Presentation conversion remains the same.

Experience has shown that both are surprisingly easy to achieve. It is really just a matter of testing different ways of handling enquiry calls, and of conducting presentations. But is testing new ways of handling enquiries and presentations risky?

Not at all. That is, not now that some KPI's have been established.

Here's why. Suppose the photographer discusses these KPI's with the team member that answers the phone, and handles enquiries. That person probably has all sorts of ideas that can possibly improve the conversion from 25% to 31% (likely significantly more than that).

And by referring to existing KPI's they can test each of those ideas, one at a time, over very short periods of time. I call these short-term tests against existing KPI's micro-tests. If the team member tries a new idea for a week and it results in a Conversion rate of 27%, then that new way will become the new standard for how enquiries are handled.

The next week the team member can try another idea and compare it to the new benchmark of a 27% conversion rate. If the test for that week generates a conversion rate less than 27%, it's eliminated. If it creates a conversion rate higher than the 27%, then this new idea becomes the new standard.

In this way it's possible to try lots of small tests with minimal or no risk. Whenever a new test results in an increase in the existing standard for any particular KPI, that tactic becomes the new standard. Whenever a test generates a KPI less than the existing standard you simply go back to using the baseline tactic.

In this way, the ultimate profit of the photographer's business can be pro-actively managed, day-to-day, and week-to-week and continually improved.

KPI's And The Art Of QuickFailing

Once you've developed an understanding of what KPI's are and how they can be used, you are in the driver's seat as far as creating a business that serves your Dream Lifestyle. And you have that desirable position because you can continually improve your business by using the QuickFailing technique.

If that sounds like something you'd rather not do, get over it.

The truth is that it's one of the most powerful ways to improve your business over any period of time. We all know from experience that we have tons of great ideas (and so does our team and our customers) that we'd love to try out - different ways of presenting our products or services; different ways of talking to our customers; different ways of attracting new customers; different ways of selling more to existing customers; and so on.

Avoid Being Held Back By Killing The Fear!

What usually holds business owners back from trying anything "different" is fear.

The fear that if something different doesn't work out there could be some serious damage done to the business. For example, you may want to raise your prices, but are still afraid (after all that you've learned so far – shame on you) that the increase will cause customers to switch to a competitor.

But by harnessing the power of KPI's you can perform many small low-risk "micro-tests" to see what the result might be. And because you are going to be measuring the impact of those tests on your KPI's you will get feedback almost instantaneously. No need to make large "bets" and wait for a relatively long time period to see what impact they have on financial performance.

KPI's allow micro-tests to be conducted over periods of time as short as a single day (or even a single hour in some cases). And in that short micro-test you will be able to get a good indication of whether the idea should be pursued further, or if it should be stopped.

Exercise – Brainstorming Your CSF's

In the space below, list as many things as you can think of that may be CSF's for your business:

_____
_____
_____
_____
_____
_____
_____
_____

Exercise – Draw Your Cycle Map To Uncover CSF's

Using the template below, draw out the Cycle Map for your business. It's a great idea to have each of your team members do it as well, and then compare them and create one that incorporates everyone's perspectives.

Our Cycle Map

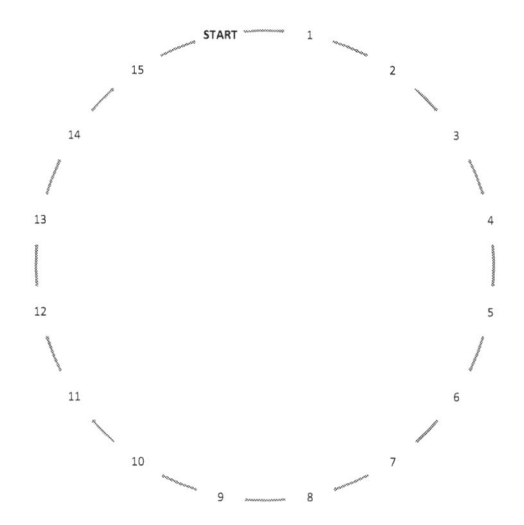

```
              START    1
         15                 2

    14                           3


  13                              4


   12                            5


         11                 6
              10        7
                  9  8
```

Exercise – Identify Your CSF's

Using your Cycle Map you have just created, identify the Critical Success Factors for your business. There should be a relatively small number of them. Four to five seems to be the most common / most workable.

In space provided next to each CSF, write a brief description / justification for why it is critical to your business and financial success.

Critical Success Factor	Justification / Explanation

Exercise – Determine Your KPI's

For each of the CSF's you identified in the previous exercise, you will now need to determine Key Performance Indicators to measure how well you are meeting those CSF's.

Use the template below to identify up to three KPI's for each CSF that will provide you with feedback about how well your business is achieving those CSF's.

For each KPI, record the current value your for that KPI as your benchmark. If you need to estimate it as a starting point that is fine.

Determine the target for each KPI that will be used to guide you as you apply QuickFailing tactics to move toward those target values.

CSF	Key Performance Indicators	Current KPI Value	KPI Target Value
_____	a) b) c)	i) ii) iii)	i) ii) iii)
_____	a) b) c)	i) ii) iii)	i) ii) iii)
_____	a) b) c)	i) ii) iii)	i) ii) iii)

————	a) b) c)	i) ii) iii)	i) ii) iii)
————	a) b) c)	i) ii) iii)	i) ii) iii)

Exercise – Identify Potential QuickFailing Tactics

Now come up with as many different tactics that you can think of for trying to move your business toward the target KPI's.

For each tactic, identify the KPI that potential QuickFailing tactic is intended to improve. Before implementing any particular QuickFailing Tactic, record the benchmark for that KPI prior to testing it, and also the resulting KPI from that QuickFailing Tactic.

That way you have an ongoing record of the QuickFailing Tactics you have identified, and what the results of each were when they were tested.

List them below:

Potential QuickFailing Tactic	KPI Targeted	Current KPI Benchmark Level	Resulting Benchmark Level

Made in the USA
Lexington, KY
16 September 2017